THE ULTIMATE TWIST

THE ULTIMATE TWIST

Suzanne Foxton

NON-DUALITY PRESS

THE ULTIMATE TWIST

First edition published March 2011 by NON-DUALITY PRESS

NON-DUALITY PRESS | PO Box 2228 | Salisbury | SP2 2GZ
United Kingdom

ISBN: 978-0-9566432-3-0

www.non-dualitypress.com

1. The Ledge

Nightfall was remarkably quick. Jason's heart sank at its efficiency. He squinted down the road, just wide enough for a vehicle; carved into the side of the mountain, uneven, with a few places once a mile or so big enough for another vehicle to pass. He supposed it was originally made for pedestrians and donkeys, so its current width was a feat of necessity-driven invention and engineering. As his range of vision lessened by the second, he despaired of ever reaching the next village. He felt a callous, insouciant Western fool, unschooled in this rough culture by merit of his disdain. Disdain was getting its comeuppance. He hoped the penalty for smugness wasn't death by misstep off the side of the unlit road.

He came to be there through laziness and incaution, however, rather than outright arrogance. His brother-in-law's father, a gentle but formidable old man, had warned him against starting his journey to the village too late in the day. Making arrangements for safe travel would have meant delays, planning, thinking. He just wanted to go, and go now. I'll walk fast, he assured Ahmed; the motivation to beat nightfall will ensure a good cardiovascular workout. Ahmed shrugged benignly. Hasid, his brother-in-law, entreated him to stay another night, but he deflected the advice good-humoredly. Janet, his sister, who knew him (and his spontaneity and recalcitrance) all too well, simply wished him a safe journey.

The light seeped away alarmingly and he got closer to the cliff wall. At last, in pitch black, he shuffled sideways, terrified but methodical. He cursed himself for an idiot. He prayed to a nebulous deity for a car to come, flooding his narrow existence on the ledge with light, rescuing him from his folly, and then amended the prayer to politely request the car not be moving too rapidly, the sudden light of the headlights perhaps a prelude to a rude plunge over the edge. A small wedge of shame intruded; how could he have done something so stupid? I'm a respected doctor, he thought. My patients depend on me. His pride and impetuousness could take a toll on them all. He went over the procedures in place to gently inform his more delicate patients of his untimely demise. Right foot, shuffle right; left foot, center. Hold the cliff face. Rachel, his PA, would phone them, and give immediate appointments with a few trusted colleagues. A very few might be admitted, so potentially damaging was the sudden death of one's psychiatrist and therapist, especially the eminent Dr. Jameson. Right foot, shuffle right. Hold the cliff wall. There was no moon to aid him.

Something crumbled. His foot shifted crazily as he cautiously sidestepped, there was open air under his left foot for a long split second; his heart raced, bathed in adrenaline. The one endless moment before his foot hit the road was delicious and pants-wettingly terrifying. There was no thought. Anything might happen; no one controlled anything; he didn't know who he was, or remember anything about his life; he became the wall he scrabbled against and the void below. At last, his foot found solid rock underneath. He rested there a few minutes, leaning on the face of the mountain. The rocks were still warm though the air was now chilly. In this ridiculous place, brought there by pride and overconfidence, the proud overconfident doctor died, if only for a moment. The ascetic teachers of the East, he thought, advocating going to the top of the mountain to meditate away the ego, had it all wrong. Go to the top of the mountain and fall off. There lies enlightenment.

Hours later, a gentle curve gave way from utter blackness to dotted fires in the valley, the light of early man, no showy twinkly electricity. His eyes embraced the light and he found he could walk relatively normally into the village, the road at last sloping into the valley. Here comes the white man in the grey salwar kameez, trying just hard enough to be native but knowing he's not fooling anyone.

And he walked; the walking seemed perfection. The tribal bonfires growing large were just right. His pride and arrogance – to be embraced. Look no further, this is paradise, he thought incongruently. This wonder cannot be improved upon.

2. The Knife

Fill the sink, move the tap far left for some nice hot water, grab the washing-up liquid, nice big squirt, watch the bubbles rise. Lovely bubbles, each tiny surface a rounded rainbow prism. Lower the stack of plates, a plate-sized hole in the bubbles; they reform, hiding the ragu smears, soon they will be clean and worthy of the family to eat off of again. Gently secrete the cutlery into the water, to the left of the plates, an old habit. Two sharp knives stay on the side. Never put a sharp knife in the dishwater: too dangerous, the beautiful bubbles would hide their presence, and perhaps then an accident, blood mingling pinkly with the diluted ragu and soapy water.

The longing, the futile amorphous yearning always there, always intense, diluted in the hot water soaking plates dangerous knives beautiful bubbles.

Wash the knives first. Take up a knife, the biggest, the most dangerous, the most expensive, the most professional. Move the tap handle all the way down with the left hand; the sink is full. Look at the knife.

It changes. It stays the same.

The knife is perfectly itself. It is so knifish; it is life, knifing. Astounding. There was never a more perfect knife. It is just as it should be, as everything is. And grasping the knife, on the floor crouching; yet nothing is crouching, there is just crouching. Boundlessness, no body, no knife, and there is a vision of swirling infinite color, in space, the birth of a perfect rainbow galaxy, spilling into a black hole and recurring, destroyed and created, winking in and out, over and over again, instantaneously, eternally, and timelessly. All of creation both here and not here. My husband comes toward me, says something, the words a nonsense but his concern registers. I assure him I'm OK in some slow exotic language, and the endless legs stretch back to the sink, and the knife/bubbles/hands are just energy, they are also utterly perfect, yet strange and unfamiliar. The knife is washed, my husband is reassured, my husband is me; his little light of awareness mingles with my own, *is* my own, that sense of me-ness is shared, its quality and essence is exactly the same as mine, that sense of aloneness, specialness, differentness, is exactly ours. The knife is carefully placed in the drying rack, and I think: it's so obvious. It's so obvious! This is how it's always been; this is how it always is. I just couldn't see it. I have been in the way of absolutely everything; and yet, I haven't.

3. The Meeting

An array of books, DVD's and CD's covered the table by the entrance to the church hall. Alistair picked one up; a book, with a mandate on the cover. *You Are All You See*, the title informed him. Am I now, he thought. He muted the derisive snort that was his automatic response to anything remotely new-agey. A couple of venerable earth mamas brushed past him; one caught his eye briefly, quizzically, and he felt the victim of mistaken identity. He wanted to go after her and tell her to keep her damned looks to herself. Their shoes were telling; one had Birkenstocks and socks, the other that kind of plain black walking shoe so many middle-aged-to-elderly women wore but which he had yet to see for sale in any shoe shop. He looked into the small crowd in the foyer, honing in on the women; not a high heel in sight. Had he missed the memo on appropriate dress for spiritual seekers? No heels, please. Any makeup must look natural. Please be sparing with hair products. All clothing must be woven from organic hemp. The men were actually more varied, a few with the "I am eccentric" uniform of cravat, umbrella/walking stick, oddly sourced suit, wavy Brylcreemed hair. Alistair suppressed a second snort. He had a powerful urge to leave. However, he was intrigued; and he also wanted to understand more about whatever life-changing phenomenon Lucy had gone through. So, he mentally held his virtual nose and marched into the hall, confidently.

Seventy-two chairs were arranged in three elegant crescents of twenty-four. One chair for the master of ceremonies faced the others; all were of the older standard church-issue folding metal variety, rather than the more modern plastic stacking type. Resigned to discomfort, he sat. In the front row he spotted some cushions on chairs saved by flyers, keys, handbags and jackets. With assured speed, he rose and claimed one from an end chair draped with a sensible navy raincoat, and returned to his less prestigious seat, anchoring the cushion under him before anyone could protest. He had a childish sense of triumph; he'd gotten away with it. There was no way he was sitting there for 1½ hours on the Church of England's best attempt at a hair shirt. He already felt a martyr for just showing up to such a ridiculous gathering of acolytes. Gentle disdain showed on his face, just enough to let people know he thought this was bullshit, yet that he was magnanimous enough to investigate it.

Lucy seemed unchanged, except that her self-destruction had slipped away. And that warranted a closer look at whatever philosophy had made this possible. According to her, the guru he'd come to see was as close as any of them ever came to whatever it was that had happened to her. So he sat back, relaxed, and committed to hearing every word with as little preconception as he could manage.

Indeterminably later, all chairs were taken, and Alistair had some serious snort-suppression issues as he observed his immediate neighbors, eyes closed, palms on thighs, feet flat on floor, and a simpering little "I am content" smile on their faces. He wondered how their nirvana would hold up if he rabbit-punched them. The guru entered, however, and no one took much notice, which surprised him. Guruji fiddled with a recording mike; the fiddling turned extravagant, and Alistair wondered if he was just the AV-knowledgeable disciple, but no, he recognized him from the blurb portrait on the books. The mike was at last in place, and guru-man went offside to fetch a glass of water. He stood in front silently for a moment, and Alistair again had an overwhelming urge to get the hell out of there. Finally, guru-dude spoke.

"Everything you've ever been looking for is right here. It is always with you. It's right here, in this room."

Oh no, thought Alistair. I have NOT been looking for these granola-eating, Earth-shoe-wearing meditators.

"In fact, what you have been searching for has never left you," continued the master.

Oh no, thought Alistair, with mock despair. I never had it in the first place.

Alistair then closed his eyes, sans the Mona Lisa smile and meditative stance. He discovered that this was like experimental theater, opera, and large boardroom meetings; the perfect opportunity for a nap. He drifted in twilight sleep, slumped on his cushion, arms crossed, until the guru-fellow became more prominent, like a radio station in the car closing in on its broadcasting source.

"Whatever it is that seems to be happening, is just perfect," soothed the master, and Alistair had to grudgingly admit that – say what you will about the guy – he had a lovely fruity voice, quite rich. He could do voiceovers. He could make car insurance sound like exactly the thing you must have.

There was a pause, and Alistair, in his sleepy semi-consciousness, was surprised by the fullness of the silence. Finally a disciple piped up with a question.

"Andy," said the questioner, and Alistair was amused at the prosaic name. "I've... " and the questioner, a woman, struggled with some overwhelming emotion. Alistair's ears pricked up. "I've been struggling with this for so long. I suppose I've come to think of it as wanting to see the truth. I was following Elwood Fee, you know him, I spent a lot of money going to see him, I read everything... and you guys all say you have the answer... but it seems like you all say different things. I'm just... so confused... " The disciple was crying. Alistair was surprised, but then he remembered Lucy's struggles with her own existential crisis; he realized he understood the woman's pain. She sighed, and continued. "I just don't understand how everybody who says they know what enlightenment is describes it so differently. How am I supposed to know what to believe?" Her last words were some of the most plaintive Alistair had ever heard. He felt anxious to hear the reply.

Without skipping a beat, Andy replied: "Everything, absolutely everything in this appearance of life, is already the immaculate expression of being. That includes everything – no exceptions. It includes all those billions of inconsistencies and irresolvable dilemmas that crop up when one story seems to intersect another.

There are so, so many stories! It includes scientific outrage at the whole idea of what we're talking about, and scientific validation by the quantum physicists. It includes the disparagement heaped upon various Advaita disciplines by various other enlightenment practices. It seems a completely chaotic bundle, a plateful of impossible choices... but whatever it is that seems to be happening, whatever it is, is perfectly and exquisitely whole.

There is nothing you can do, except what you do; and there is nothing you are supposed to believe. The confusion you feel – there's nothing wrong with it. There is a strong desire to get the story just right, and there is nothing wrong with that either. Despite the appearance of so many stories, there are no stories.

Stories need time to happen, and there is no time. In fact there is nothing at all, despite the appearance of vast space and tiny atomic activity and Fred, the nosy neighbor next door." Smattering of laughter.

"The deepest reality, the absolute source, awareness, oneness, whatever you care to call it, Jehoshaphat or maybe even God," gentle laughter again, "appears as all these conflicting stories and thoughts and teachings. It's the biggest thing in this room. It's the only thing in this room.

There is no need to detach, or self-inquire – like Elwood likes to ask you to do – or be the stillness, or know yourself completely, although these apparent actions can come up. You are already one. You are already complete. Whatever it is that seems to need to be done will be done. It unfolds flawlessly despite the flaws, unblemished despite the warts. There is no one who needs help to be this perfection; you are already that. Perhaps that's the only thing you need to believe."

There was another pause, and despite the surface profundity of the words just spoken, Alistair wasn't impressed by the quality of the silence this time.

What a load of bollocks, he thought.

4. The Breakdown

I have no respite here on the sofa, in the same position, prone, feet up, as nearly always. It is a Herculean task to get up and use the toilet; each step up the stairs exhausts me. Eating is similarly draining; my digestive system is all wrong, there is pain, and any small sustenance like a yogurt is either vomited or goes through unchanged. A small glass of glucose water is all I can manage, one hopeless sip at a time. I feel almost nothing. Even the craving for the pills, the codeine that keeps me from hell, is muted. The futile, constant longing for death is at bay. My shame cannot be allowed, so overwhelming is its power; so what's left is a numb nothing.

Alistair comes in the front door, click kerchunk, and appears beside the sofa.

"I think it's time we did something," he says, determined but wary, not sure if I'll carry on with the cover story of amoebic dysentery, recently acquired in Egypt, our less-than-satisfactory summer holiday, marred by Mum's drinking and pill-taking and general mental absence. "Let's get you to the hospital," he ventures. I don't care what happens anymore.

So, unable to walk, I am carried to the car, all 6 stone (80 pounds, 50 kilos) of me. After some indeterminate interim I slide into a bony chair at the hospital where a nurse takes my history and some blood. The game is up. The truth of my drug abuse comes out. Eighty-eight pills a day, in four 22 pill dosages; 22,000mg each of paracetamol and ibuprofen to get to the 1200 or so mg of codeine; in the end, each pill is swallowed singly, then every ounce of my will is called upon to keep it in my body; swallow, swallow, sip of water, swallow swallow swallow, until the urge to vomit is overcome. I am a wreck. Pain radiates from my poor ulcerated stomach. Soon I am in a bed and hooked up to potassium, glucose and a blood transfusion. Alistair leaves to tell the children that their mother's self-hatred has put her in hospital, although he probably doesn't phrase it just that way. Ever the survivor, I want a book, the television, a cigarette. I get my phone and text another mother from the school that I can't be where I'm meant to be when I'm meant to be there, doing whatever chore I'm meant to do. A doctor appears. "You should be dead," he says. The blood work shows a hemoglobin level below that of what is usually a corpse. I feel great self-pity, in its finest, most loving form; a little compassion for the suffering me; why can't I actually *be* a corpse? Why does my ridiculously robust body continue to live? Why does it cling to life when anyone else's would have succumbed? The yearning for a book, the television, a cigarette is just a masked longing to die, a constant companionable feeling that something is missing.

I am missing. There isn't any coherent story; it is shattering as the opiates creep from my system. There is just muted cacophony, jumbled sights/sounds/sensations, trouble mixed with guilt stirred by despair. The story of Lucy, the papery, flimsy top layer, the persona, the wife/mother/production designer, chairperson of the PTA, able and proficient, is revealed to be just that – a story, thin as the skin of an onion; peeling, flaky, brown and ugly. Everything is wrong. Even the brief release of sleep doesn't come; the opiate withdrawal sees to that.

Alistair comes back. We speak. There is to be no divorce. Again, despite my appallingly self-centered behavior, that of an addict in active addiction, Alistair is willing to stick around and see what happens. Remorse is all I feel; at least it's something. Helpless, all-encompassing remorse at a behemoth I can't control.

It isn't long before I can wheel my drip down a long corridor, take the lift down four floors, wheel the drip down an even longer corridor, go outside into the freezing September sun and smoke. I am slightly elated. The hell is subsiding. It isn't just the itch of the nicotine craving, scratched; it is survival. I should be dead, I think, and smile... and remember. How many mornings have I awakened, still alive, to impossible bleakness accompanied by the thought Oh God, not another day to get though? How many nights before have I swallowed every pill in the house to be greeted in the morning, ears singing with the tinnitus of an aspirin overdose, to the grim sentence of another day of life? Warily, I poke the despair with a mental stick, the way a naturalist pokes a sleeping cobra. Why do I feel this way? Why do I want to die? Why am I in so much pain and despair? Easy enough to write it off as the remorse and regret of a recently clean addict, disgusted by their own actions, which mandate violation of the moral code. It is that, but I realize there is more. There's more to it. Maybe there's a reason I keep taking chemicals to subdue – well, everything, and this last time after seven years of being clean and sober. Maybe, as they say in the 12-step rooms, some secret is keeping me sick.

A layer of defense peels painfully, briskly away, like a barely healed scab.

5. The Warm Bed

Jason enjoyed the cultural tradition of men hugging when they meet. He was squeezed into a powerful one, at last standing by one of the fires that had so elated him on the ledge. Several men, all in their thirties, all drinking tea, all in salwar kameez, were energetically thrumming with subdued excitement, curiosity and veiled distaste at his appearance out of the blackness. They sat on a collection of folding chairs and purpose-formed stones, their discussion of freedom and imprisonment happily interrupted. He was given a lawn chair, the best chair by its fairly unripped look. Jason also enjoyed the reverence of age and experience; in a group of thirty-somethings, fifty was venerable. His premature grey was also an asset. He knew better than to disclose to them that he was a doctor; while visiting his sister, he had realized that being a doctor inspired reverence only until they learned he was a psychiatrist.

Water appeared, and he drank, suddenly thirstier than he ever had been; the water seemed more like water than any water he had ever drunk. The tea that appeared next seemed the perfect drink, warming his cold and turgid gut. He relaxed. Most of the men had appreciable English and he told his tale of the ledge, emphasizing his newfound humility, wishing to be accepted. They appreciated his candor. Female eyes peered at him from the window of the nearest dwelling – the tea maker – and he was careful not to stare in the direction of the window, respecting the taboo against looking too closely at women. He was under this stricture even with his own sister; during his visit, his sister's father-in-law had frowned constantly in disapproval at their easy familiarity.

After some sympathetic feedback and a low-voiced conference punctuated, to Jason's ears, with derisive laughter, he was dispatched to one of the men's houses – Hakim's – where he was given a basin and a jug of water. He undressed and sank gratefully onto the bed, after scrubbing fitfully at his rancid armpits. The bed radiated the warmth of a recently displaced occupant. He was too tired, and too immersed in the immediacy of his body's needs, to feel guilty. Sleep was instant.

6. The Busker

There was no need to tell Lucy that he had fallen asleep at the Advaita meeting. He had seen and heard enough to grasp that the guy wasn't a robed Hindu-style white guru, with bankrupt devotees and a Bentley outside for him to drive home to his country mansion in. In fact, Alistair hadn't even paid the ten pounds to get in; he hadn't avoided it on purpose, but there was no one collecting when he happened to enter and the admission charge wasn't policed. He could admire that; they didn't seem at all avaricious. But it just wasn't his thing. All that stuff about whatever happens is perfect – what nonsense. Sure, there's nothing wrong with accepting your lot in life, but it wasn't the right message for the ambitious of this world, and he was ambitious. Regardless of his opinion, he bought the latest book on his way out; again, it was reasonably priced. He still wanted to understand where Lucy was coming from. Things were good, and he loved her; he felt it his duty to know what it was that had helped her, that had stopped the wanton self-destruction and all the collateral damage within the family.

Because, he thought sadly, it wasn't me. He had really wanted it to be him, and the family. He wanted to be her savior.

Home, he told Lucy the meeting had given him a lot of food for thought, and she was impressed at his open-mindedness when he showed her the book.

"I'll be surprised if you read even one page," she told him, wise to his ways.

Well, that was the kind of challenge he responded to and she knew it.

The family had carried on in good shape in his absence. He was reasonably reassured that Lucy hadn't just dropped all the rules and let the kids go nuts on the games and television. He had blipping radar for the children of his peers, and their habits and disciplines; he worked hard for the school fees; he wanted them to have every opportunity to be professionals, with the drive and self-governance that being an Oxbridge scholar took. He was threatened by Lucy's contentment, and acceptance. Although they were laudable human qualities, he felt he had to step in and help the family to the next level of achievement, and happiness. Being a good parent meant letting your children go, and loving them no matter what their choices and mistakes; but he was going to make sure they made as few mistakes as possible before they left the shelter of his roof.

On the subway the next day, on his way to a weekend business meeting, on a line not associated with too many tourist destinations, making it nicely empty on a Saturday, he opened the book at random.

'In this beautiful, ugly, chaotic, orderly, ambiguous and pointless adventure most label reality, duality itself is the only point. Duality is oneness, apprehending itself. And that is the meaning, the secret of life: it exists. The fragile constructs that make nothingness a solid table or an overwhelming feeling are the miracles. The appearance, the mere fact that anything exists at all, is stunning, and awesome. Look carefully at the very nature of matter, and there is nothing there. What looks, changes it; ask any particle physicist. Where there is no one, no choice, no

thing at all, whatever unfolds, unfolds in unspeakable freedom. The persistent arising of choices and dilemmas and challenges are the joys of duality. Whatever their conclusion, however heartbreaking or enchanting, is unimportant; there is no one to shepherd the journey, no goal that exists other than to fulfill itself, for itself. Don't despair if this isn't seen. If the journey still seems remarkably important, if the character you play isn't seen to be every character and everything, life still unfolds just as it must, whether "you" feel better or not. Feeling better may indeed seem to be the goal, but if it is pursued, you are not pursuing. There are no mistakes, including thoughts that there are, indeed, dreadful mistakes. The task of letting go, so desperately desired, is difficult when the thing that lets go is the thing that needs to be let go of. In fact, it is impossible. But letting go may seem to happen. There is nothing an idea can do to dispel itself. So if there still seems to be time, for want of anything better to do, pursue whatever goal it is that presents itself; there are no mistakes.'

What a load of old twaddle, thought Alistair.

An illegal one-stop busker embarked at Mornington Crescent, annoying Alistair before he strummed a single chord. "Good afternoon, ladies and gentlemen, don't feel obliged to pay me, I only do this for the captive audience," he began affably and launched into the blues. He was strolling past the braced and tense Alistair, who managed to discern the lyrics:

"... heard a voice, had no choice
Needed to be free."

Unimpressed by the synchronicity of it, it occurred to him that Lucy would be similarly unimpressed, but amused.

He ran after the departing busker and gave him a pound coin just as he was about to step off the carriage.

"Mind the gap," Alistair reminded him. The busker rewarded him with a bemused and grateful smirk.

7. The Case History

That summer we visit Cairo and the experiential height is riding horses near the pyramids. Fate graces me with a brilliant horse. Reins in my right hand, he turns at the least indicative pull; just a small nudge with my heels and he canters, happily controlled, and we zigzag across the sand around Max and Florrie on their lesser nags, who are gentle and reluctant for speed; and around Alistair, perched on his comic camel. The pyramids have their otherworldly golden haze, bizarrely pointed in a world given to boxes. A moment more perfect than most, yet it isn't enough. I canter far enough away to blur my actions and swallow the ten pills I have nestled in my pocket for this moment; swallow, swallow, swallow until the gag reflex abates. Then I guiltily canter back to Alistair and remark, as naturally as possible, on the beauty of the circumstances as I wave to the children. I hate myself, yet am elated that I get away with it.

At work, filming, I watch the monitor, and spot the boom mike drifting into the square of filmed reality on the top left. Then I stop filming a moment later when "XIT" comes into frame (3/4 of EXIT when the sign above the door should say SALIDA, as the scene takes place in Spain); momentarily free, I run off to the tiny hallway outside the underground storage unit we're filming in and down 22 pills at once washed down by a huge slug of diet cola. There is that elation, the sense of having fooled 'em again.

Soon, the cola would have vodka in it. The vodka mercifully speeds up my body's collapse.

I lie in the hospital bed, drips in place, and relentlessly remember the worst parts of the relapse: being at the school fair, helping set up the strawberries and cream stall, suggesting they move under a tree, and then dashing to the bathroom to force down a huge handful of pills. Because it is time. Because the levels have to be topped up. And more recently, putting stage makeup on 30 year-six children, dashing off to the swimming pool to take my son's forgotten swimsuit to him, taking a surreptitious slug of Baileys in the car and waking up at 6pm – past time to collect the children. Max's class has marched past me, passed out, on the way back to the school. I hurry home woozily to make up another lie that can't be easily checked. My husband, called from work to pick up the kids, believes me because he wants to. Then I go into the kitchen to take another handful of pills.

I lie in the hospital bed, dying of shame. The remorse I had thus far avoided is here; so is the impotent wish that I could take it back (often labeled "regret"), just go back into the time line and change it; or, more realistically, just die. I lie in the hospital bed and long for death. I want it so. I'm not so shallow as to not want to face the consequences of the active addiction, I just hate myself. I don't deserve life, I keep spitting on its miracle. Lying there, I realize that life is too hard, and again remember that each morning stretching back into childhood I wake up and think: another day to get through.

Alistair comes and sits on the side of the bed. He is confused.

"Is this why you wanted a divorce?" he asks, referring to my not-so-secret relapse, and I go red with shame. How can I have blocked all that out? I asked him for a divorce a few weeks ago. I suggested moving out. I remember looking for nearby apartments, barely able to make it up a flight of stairs in my frailty, explaining to the waiting agent that I was just getting over flu. A space of my own was the ostensible goal; truly, I was no longer able to tolerate Alistair and his relentless interference with my self-destruction. The children, I realize, were the real motivation; they mustn't bear witness to the inevitable decline and degradation. Some unfamiliar tears cross the barrier. I'm afraid to be alone.

"I never really wanted a divorce," I say.

"Neither did I," he replies. I think: he's crazy. Why would he want to be with me? I'm shit. But the relief is enormous.

Alistair walks slowly and thoughtfully out to the waiting Max and Florrie.

"Mummy's probably going to be in the hospital for a while", he says. "But we're not going to get a divorce".

Why, why, why did he have to be so abrupt? I can hear them in the hallway. The children mewl and coo ecstatically. Their fractured world would hold together for at least a little longer.

Back in the bed I remember sitting them down a week earlier and telling them about the impending separation. Alistair and I hold hands, try to soften the blow, say we still love each other but can't live together. They surprise us by talking about it, spontaneously, to their classmates and teachers. How can the progeny of my broken, inauspicious life be so mentally healthy? After this new news, they joyfully tell their friends the divorce is no longer imminent. The three classmates whose parents remain apart doubtless nurse unconscious grudges. How can I die now when they expect life to be perfect again? Or at least, lived out in a nuclear family? The thought of plowing back into it all, the fray of life, where every task is Herculean and every moment wretched, deepens my desolation. I lie in the hospital bed. I lie in the despair. My mind spins. What can I do? Where can I go from here? I long for wholeness, but not seriously. More hopefully, I long for spontaneous death.

8. The Boy with Bloody Feet

The old Colonel was a treat Jason hadn't expected on this trip. A proper vestige of the Empire, he had many stories about the teething pains of Pakistan, the horrors of Partition, and his evidently crucial role in its implementation. He described the makeshift hospitals and jury-rigged infrastructure with a rich voice and the polish of a well-paid after dinner speaker. A respite from the relentless present, he brought back the Pakistan of the frontier, always churning under the chain of various factions and warlords. After so many years, the people seemed resigned to unrest.

Colonel Miller held court, regaling a satisfied audience every time. So many stories. Jason abruptly took his leave from the extended breakfast and walked the streets of the village, not such an untouched place after all. He was freshly washed, dressed and victualed, and hoped to bump into his saviors of the night before, who had delivered him to the hotel very early that morning on their way to whatever livelihood they eked. He wandered into the market and was entranced by the rugs, the shine, the heat, the spiciness, the undercurrent of rotting garbage, and the jumbled yet organized mélange. The people barely noticed him, gray hair and European demeanor notwithstanding. This was for tourists too, they were common, but the money wasn't made from them disproportionately so he wandered relatively unmolested. He stopped at a marquee full of bowls of apricots, where shoppers could sit and rest with a cup of tea. A stool was proffered and he sat in the shade. The crowd slowly rumbled and shuffled around him. All his receptors were turned to max. Never was yellowy-orange such an entity unto itself, screaming from the bowls of fruit.

At the feet of the Colonel that evening, after a quick call to Wimbledon to assure his sardonic wife he was, indeed, still alive after nearly plunging off the cliff into the void, Jason was again treated by the master storyteller.

"You wouldn't believe the conditions," Colonel Miller croaked, his plummy elderly tones so fit for the job. "There was no sanitation, no plumbing, no transport, nothing at all. We had to build about 14 villages up from scratch. The natives, they were willing, surprisingly so, in fact they were dead keen to get a new Islamic country up and running, but they were exhausted. The kiddies were all half-dead from the journey and beside themselves from what they'd seen. Shell-shocked. A lot of them needed some real medical attention. Well, there was a hospital of sorts. We weren't even supposed to be there, you know, but our commanding officer was a bit of a maverick, always found a way to be where he thought we ought to be whether the boys back home thought so or not. This time our transport supposedly missed us. So we had another evac coming, you see, and everything we did was on borrowed time. So he had us doing everything, our medic was just about half-dead himself, flying around headless-chicken style, trying to triage the sick, but it wasn't even called triage then; just plain common sense, you know, who needed help most. My job was rounding up any stragglers. I found a family about three miles short of the mark with a broken cart. They were in bad shape but they were stubborn; they weren't going to leave this cart, it was everything they owned, their whole life. So I got the young man of the family, I forget what his name was, to play wheel, and he held up one side while the rest of us grabbed what we could and played pack horse. We didn't stop, just a steady pace, momentum and adrenaline was keeping us going. I don't mind telling you that I wasn't in much better shape than the family after about a mile or so, I took most of the weight, only because I was fittest. Well, we trundled on and each step was hell, we were all quiet, just getting on with it. The picture of grim determination. I have to say that when I spotted the outskirts of the new village I was bloody relieved, another quarter mile would have done me in. And no telling what level of extremity the family was in. We stopped and the medic was right on the young man, carrying him over his shoulder although there wasn't much to Dr. Arnold himself. I saw his feet as the doctor carried him away; they were bloody shreds. Just raw meat."

The Colonel savored this part, the emotion blanketing him, the fruits of a good story properly honored with a pause. "Never seen anything like it. He never made a sound. His mother, well, she was hysterical when she saw the state of her son's feet. Looked at the cart of belongings like she'd never seen it before, and didn't care if she ever saw it again." He settled back, letting go of his gift of the tale, enjoying the reaction of the group of ten or so hotel guests, mostly English, privileged to avail themselves of one of Colonel Miller's slices of early Pakistani life.

"I'm off, Colonel, thank you for a memorable evening," announced Jason formally, and he trooped off to a bed so decadently comfortable that, this time, he actually did feel guilty; for what, he wasn't sure. The guilt didn't keep him awake.

An abrupt pincer-grip on his arm woke him; it didn't feel much later than when he'd retired. The Colonel was an inch from his ear, smelling of cigars and dentures.

"The Taliban chappies are looking for you, I'm reasonably sure," he hissed loudly. "I've liberated your passport from the front desk. They're out there, asking after an English shrink. You should slip out. You don't want to be caught if you're on their list."

"What on Earth do they want with me?" asked Jason, blearily wary.

"Who knows? Does it matter? Come along, here, I've thrown whatever was in your drawers into your pack." He shoved the rucksack at Jason and hauled him out of bed. "Dress sharpish. Come on, quiet now," he complained as Jason lumbered clumsily into his massive salwar trousers. One end of the drawstring had burrowed into the seam channel. He fumbled with it, but it was a task requiring patience, rescuing the buried cord, so the Colonel whipped the belt out in one motion and used it outside the trousers. Jason felt like a trusting child; fear and excitement were waking him up. The Colonel finished trussing his waist and Jason pulled on the kameez.

"Good enough," rasped Colonel Miller. "Now, Dr. Jameson, for your covert mission." They padded through the dark, aromatic, wood-paneled halls, the Colonel in regulation camel slippers, Jason barefoot and carrying his Keen walking sandals. There was no room for anything but the task at hand. Jason felt little resistance, surprisingly. Here was life, unjudged, just lived.

"Here we are," announced the Colonel as they made it through to the far side of the dark and sumptuous kitchens where a swinging slatted wooden door offered escape. "Off you go. Here, cover your head when you get some distance." He handed Jason a bundle that seemed a simple roll of white cloth, a turban if properly maneuvered. "Just climb over that low wall. Straight through to the main road. Walk just off it until light. Hitch a ride when you can to the airport. And just leave," he ordered sternly. "You can phone your family when you're back in England. Here, here," he harrumphed, reconsidering, and got a pen and napkin from the waiter's station. "Jot down your wife's number and I'll advise her.

Don't call anyone. Just get the bloody hell out of here. Off you go." Jason had the presence of mind, or the instinct, to stand at attention and salute the Colonel. Pleased, he saluted back. "Yes yes yes that's all very well," said the Colonel gruffly. "Off you go." Jason was rudely shoved out the door. He missed some stacked scrap by a millimeter. Not looking back, he heaved his middle-aged bulk over the low wall, and, again by moonlight, toured Pakistan.

Just walk, thought Jason, don't think. His family, his patients, his safety, his survival, his life, all faded away. His values, his ethical code, his morning routine, his career path, all melted into the nothingness they were; just thoughts, mere electrical sparks. Everything he ever valued, everything he ever thought was important, was eclipsed by the moonlit escape. He had seen no Taliban. He had heard nothing; the hotel had been the silent nightscape it always was after 11:30. He imagined them, bearded, severe, ripe with body odor – even by Pakistani standards – standing at the front desk, demanding to see everyone's passports; yet for all he knew the Colonel was bored and loony, creating a drama to add to his repertoire of anecdotes. The roll of cloth for a turban hung in loops around his arm; come to think of it, he didn't remember seeing too many men wearing turbans in Pakistan. The headgear might make him a sure target. He might very well have been delivered unto the proverbial hunt for the undomesticated waterfowl.

Jason didn't care. In fact, not caring didn't even occur to him. He was running, yet *Jason* wasn't running. Everything was running.

9. The Survivor

The doctors come, they stand at the foot of the bed, a consultant and a bevy of junior doctors, clipboards clasped to their chests.

"Hmmm," says the consultant, looking at my chart. "Ahhh, this is the one I was talking about."

"The duodenal ulcer?" asks a junior.

"Yes," says the consultant.

"Has a mental health consultation been recommended?" asks another junior.

"Mrs. Naughton," says the consultant, ignoring the indelicate question and addressing not me but an interesting case, "has someone been to speak to you about what you've been doing to yourself?"

"Not yet," I reply, in Good Girl mode. I *need* to be helpful.

"You're a very lucky woman," he says without a hint of irony. "You should be dead. See," he addresses the enrapt mini-throng, "her hemoglobin was at 4.3 when she arrived. Not only was she alive, she was conscious and lucid." I mentally dispute both those states but say nothing. "At what level of g/dl can we expect mortality?" he asks, remembering he's meant to be teaching these people.

"About 4.5?" ventures a junior.

"It varies, but yes," says the learned doctor.

I should be dead. Yes, I should be dead. The juniors are looking at me, impressed at my hardiness, and puzzled by it. My body is a rock. My will to live lives. I feel cheated, and resigned.

10. The Argument

"Wow," said Lucy, as Alistair displayed the book to her. "I'm impressed. I really am," she assured him, with a little bit of unfeigned awe. "I never thought you'd even go to one of these things, much less buy a book." They knew each other's characters so well, and tolerated each other so completely, that even surprises were accepted absolutely. Her observation was delivered with an arch tone and a wryly raised eyebrow that said "nothing you can do will ever put me off."

"I read a bit on the subway," he boasted, buying into her tone.

"So what do you think?" she asked.

"That it's a load of new-age hippie claptrap," he monotoned.

"Just when I was harboring hopes for your personal growth and development," she moaned, with unfelt sorrow.

"Oh, there's no hope for that," he replied cheerfully. "Stuck in my ways. Forever conservative and cynical. Completely beyond hope."

"The very thing that attracted me to you," she said, rewarding his mock intractability with a big hug.

They took the kids to a water park that afternoon and enjoyed the slides and the wave machine just as much as they did. Alistair noted the careful way Lucy discarded her towel at the pool's edge, never allowing humanity to glimpse her bare legs, which childbearing had marked with thread veins and varicosities. Didn't an enlightened person not care anymore what others thought? Filled with the liberation of the soul, didn't they unblinkingly and carelessly let it all hang out, each flaw in its full glory, loving every bit of their body and self, enticing the rest of the world to do the same? Apparently not.

Later, the children were allowed their precious evening time in front of their technology, Skyping and MSN-ing and gaming and YouTubing away. Alistair and Lucy had their quality time together in the sitting room. This was often a film too raunchy for an 11- and 13-year-old, but tonight, Lucy asked, "Why don't you open your new book at random and read some?"

"Aloud?" asked Alistair.

"Oh yes please," enthused Lucy, wry brow working.

With ceremony, he fetched the book, sat reverently, closed his eyes and did some "ohming" for Lucy's amusement as he thumbed the pages. Predictably, she enjoyed it. With a flourish, he opened the book and read:

'While the dreamer still dreams of being separate, it is anathema to even think of leaving it all behind. The idea that everything you ever believed in, everything you ever valued, and all the treasures of life mean nothing is very hard to take. The separate self will do a lot not to die. Yet paradoxically, this separate self is just oneness, separate-selfing. This is beyond any idea of right and wrong, or good and evil. Yet all the complex and dark, twisted paths that individuals seem led down by their (often immutable) beliefs are just as they should be, and are as meaningless as anything else. Purpose may arise, but there is no purpose to life. Meaning may come up, but life, as a story, is meaningless. The meaning is a shining, obvious thing, the salient quality of everything that seems to manifest. My little *dream-self knows he is dreaming, but the dream unfolds very much as it always did, with perhaps less trouble, and certainly what trouble there is remains unclaimed. Strangely, the values and the way I live seem more useful, but this is not the goal; there is no goal. There is no one who could have a goal, and if a goal arises, the apparent process of attaining it or perhaps failing to is sweet in its playful, intrinsically fulfilling nature. Even bitterness, short-lived, is notably apropos. I seem to remember a tumbling feeling of despair when I realized that the ups and downs of my seemingly extraordinary life were empty; yet in their emptiness, they were somehow even more profound. Yet any memories that seem to come up, rather than proving time's existence, belie it; any memory is a memory remembered now. All the good and all the bad I thought that I had done is of nothing. And all the good and bad that seem to arise are different faces of unconditional love.'*

Alistair stopped and was silent. He was angry. He certainly hoped Lucy didn't buy into all this errant nonsense.

"He puts it well," said Lucy innocently, filling the gap.

" 'He puts it well'? What do you mean he puts it well? What a load of horseshit. How can you say that? What the fucking hell am I working my ass off for? Why are we sacrificing our retirement for the kids' education? This crap is dangerous. It encourages laziness. It encourages every weak-minded person to give up, and not do anything with their lives. To stop working towards a goal, to give up on their dreams. Is that you? Do you think everything we're working for is meaningless?" He noticed he had vacated his seat and was towering over her, brandishing the book for emphasis.

Lucy looked up at him, surprised. "W-e-e-ll," she said cautiously, "I think what he's saying is that life is even bigger than our goals and what we work for. And that maybe goals are of value because, um, not because of the goal, but that everything is, um, of equal value, or something. Hey, Alistair," she soothed, "hey, I'm here. I'm with you. Nothing's changed just because you read some passage in a book. We're working together, like always. Better even. It's fine."

"It is not fine." He tossed the book on the sofa as if it was a maggoty piece of meat. "I surely hope you don't believe this bullshit. Because I'm done worrying about you. I've had it with you being the wild card in all this. You're the big danger, you know. You're the one who can take everything we've worked for and flush it down the toilet. It's bad enough you're an addict and alcoholic. Now, I expect you to pack up and move to some commune where they all meditate and grow vegetables. Chant on their hemp mats because they can't hack it, because life's too much of a challenge. Great. Just fantastic." He was sitting again, and less confrontational; Lucy felt safe enough that the sardonic eyebrow was again raised and ready.

"He certainly pushed your buttons," she said, and got up to check that the kids weren't downloading porn or being groomed by a pedophile posing as a 14-year-old paraplegic schoolgirl.

He was calmer. There he sat; palms on knees, lit by the art deco hood-ornament-lady lamp, and Lucy watched him from the doorway, appraising his mood. It was touch and go. She used to take any criticism or disagreement as a possibility that Alistair might not love her anymore. Now, it didn't matter. She could, it seemed, bear anything, weather any storm; but perhaps there wasn't any storm to weather.

11. The Admission

Alistair and I are in the waiting area of one of the psychiatric consultants at our local mental hospital. We make the drive in semi-silence, punctuated occasionally by "I'm so sorry," from me. I feel I am drowning in shame, but also protectively detached. I'd been in this hospital before, in rehab, a few years ago. Now, here I am again, all that money and effort a waste. The consultant, the same one I had in rehab, approaches. He is gentle, and kindly asks me into his office. I feel sorry for Alistair, watching me disappear, not privy to the sacred communications between patient and shrink. We sit across from one another. The therapy posture, very formal, face to face, seems impossibly contrived. I want to rush into his arms, but it's just not allowed.

"So, tell me," he starts.

"I don't know," I reply, feeling small. "I guess I'm trying to kill myself. I feel like I can't cope with anything. I just want some quiet for a while." I don't feel I'm saying anything useful.

"Do you feel as if you want to kill yourself now?" he asks, the Good Shrink with the Next Right Question.

"I haven't got the energy," I say. It's true.

We have one of those pregnant pauses that punctuate therapy.

"Do you think you can help me?" I ask. It's plaintive.

"I will do everything I can, and then some," he says.

"Do I have to be in with the addicts again?" I ask. It seems redundant. I know all about rehab. I know how to stay sober. But none of it means anything if I don't give a shit.

"Oh, no-o-o-o," he says, dismissive. "We'll put you in a nice quiet wing." Yes, I think, the "Shh, don't disturb them, you might upset them" wing.

We have another shortish pause, shot with relief.

"Do you think I can have a hug?" I ask, abruptly, risking rejection early on so as to get it over with.

"Of course you can," he replies, carelessly tossing boundaries out the window. We rise and hug – I have to struggle out of the chair, weak and pathetic – and he goes out to tell Alistair the good news: I should stay in hospital for a couple of weeks, at least.

Alistair travels home, leaving me to it.

12. The Flight

Jason walked boldly along the road in breaking dawn, feeling he wasn't a big enough of a fish to have to hide, doubting the existence of a Taliban contingent that could possibly be interested in him, yet not resenting the Colonel for chucking him out merely to re-inject a little drama into his life. He thought indulgently of a few of his patients, addicts, the kind who needed a great deal of stimulation, who escaped whatever inner realities they couldn't face by stirring up their outer story; a grudge-trumped-up-to-a-war here, a family-gathering-turned-crisis there. He understood, he sympathized, hell, he even identified. That urge to stir it all up was not a million miles away from his own desire to visit his sister in turbulent Pakistan, to brave the pitch black cliff, to run into the night on the word of a possibly delusional man. And it was working. This was being alive. He cared little of consequences. He cared little for a constructed life that seemed so distant, and if not empty, unimportant.

A truck approached from the other direction and passed in a cloud of dust and gravel. As it approached, there was a delicious fear; just untethered fear, without obvious cause.

He walked and walked, planless, musing about the Taliban and their reputation in the West. Evil bearded stinking fundamentalist misguided fanatics. So blind they would blow up a peaceful, enormous, historic Buddha to smithereens. So frightened of the open, yielding, nurturing side of humanity they can't forgive women for being female, and open, and nurturing. The enemy needed for the reinforcement of Western values. Even the most liberal, open-hearted, mentally healthy altruist disliked them. And now, even if in some fantasy, they were after *him*.

An early rising farmer walked past, nodded. Jason nodded back. His head was turbaned to the best of his ability. Having no mirror or experience, he could only guess it looked a right mess.

What does the farmer think of the Taliban, he wondered. Like most people, he probably just hoped he could get on with the business of surviving, that the rules were neither too strict nor anarchic, that he and his family could cope with the formidable challenges that life presented even in the cushion of a reasonably benign government. That his daughters and sons married well, and learned the lessons taught by having their own children. That in vulnerable old age they were neither ignored nor too much of a burden, or if they did need care, that they would accept their necessity and learn those lessons of humility, too. That death would be neither too fearful nor too painful. All the classic conditions of humanity, which the families of the Taliban must also share, being human. The farmer probably hoped that no one, Taliban or not, interfered with him too much.

On the subject of villains, Jason thought of Hitler, his easily diagnosed megalomania and paranoid delusions, his childhood of abuse and neglect affecting the next generation to some unimaginably exponential degree. Then a colleague of his came to mind, a psychiatrist known for over-prescribing psychoactive drugs to his patients. When a junior doctor in his hospital told one of the colleague's patients that he didn't need to take quite such a huge dosage of whatever-it-was, his esteemed colleague did what he could, through writing letters to the General Medical Council, to smear the junior's budding reputation. Jason wrote some letters of his own, restoring the junior's promise and future career. He remembered relating this story to one of his patients, and the patient opining it was sad that Jason's colleague felt so threatened that he had to destroy the source of the mere *hint* that his pharmacological practices were over-zealous. Jason became annoyed. "How sad it was that Hitler was so fucked up he had to orchestrate the deaths of millions," he told the patient, who was somewhat taken aback. Now that Jason was a victim (even if only in fantasy) of human fear and xeno-phobia gone mad, that anger was gone. He saw it all: Hitler here, Gandhi there; the junior doctor balancing his col-league; the selfless mothers of the world and their nurturing energies answering the sweeping avarice of corporations. He suspected that it all cancelled each other out, and we were left with what we started with: nothing. Nothing displaying itself in a vast playground.

A car roared by behind him, and without thinking he turned and waved them down. The dust revealed a Humvee, sand camo and helmets. The American Army pulled over to rescue him.

13. The Worst Thing

The hug had been promising and bore fruit relatively quickly. Between three enormous meals a day, which absorbed easily into the latest healed ulcer, I am in his office, revealing a bit of remorseful behavior here, waxing resignedly about addiction there. Three weeks later, in my room, cross-legged on the bed, I shuffle through some old papers Alistair had brought from home; the Keep Box. A mysterious postcard showing the Golden Gate Bridge drops out. With angry, thick, indented black text, nearly illegible, it reads:

> Lu,
>
> You bitch. How could you not have told me?
> After all I confided in you about my baby?
>
> Don't ever get in touch with me again.
>
> Harriet
> P.S. **_Bitch._**

"I drank and drugged through my pregnancy with Max," I tell Jason later that day. He is at his stoic best. Unfazed – that was the quality and essence of his being.

"It's the worst thing I've ever done. Well, it's what I feel worst about," I continue, matter-of-fact in tone if not in disposition. There is a pause, crackling with energy. "I found a postcard from my friend Harriet who didn't approve of me at all," I say, sadly. "It jogged my memory."

"Now that you've started, it's like removing the offending log from a logjam. Everything will follow," Jason observes sagely.

"I believe you, Jason," I say, calling him by name for the first time.

Musing about using his name briefly deflects a tidal surge of memory. So this is PTSD, a disembodied and bemused voice notes. Then I am reliving sitting on the edge of my bed, bump containing Max swollen below my heavy breasts, taking a Vicodin and washing it down with wine, cursing my child, wishing him dead. Not because of some worthy-ish reasons of an unplanned pregnancy, but simply because Max is interfering with my using. He makes me have to hide it, to ameliorate it, to regret it. A memory surge of bewilderment at my own actions engulfs me here, in the comfy therapy-chair, which is now the edge of the bed. I can smell the medicinal tang of Vicodin, taste the wine at the back of my tongue. The light from the window in my flashback, bright late summer light, is oddly similar to the yellow walls in Jason's office. Finally, this is what I have blocked for so long; the utter despair, the self-loathing, the baffling inability to stop what I'm doing. How can I do this to Max? Black bewilderment, relived or perhaps lived for the first time, nearly drowns me; and such terror, such fear of what I'll give birth to in a couple of months' time. Self-hatred beyond description. The knot just below my ribs, the held-in emotion, loosens abruptly and unexpectedly; it has been there for months; if I can only cry, if I can only let it out, but evidently I don't deserve to. I come to and notice I am sobbing, and that Jason has traversed the sacred space between us and is holding me. He maternally strokes my hair, presses his cheek to my back, kisses the back of my head. I slowly rise, dry my tears with a sleeve, and snivel for a bit. Jason disengages himself and retreats to his throne.

"You've really begun now," he says. "Get some rest." We rise and he gives me a super-hug, lifting me off the ground. Stunned, I make the short journey back to my room, fall face forward on the bed, and sleep for three hours.

I wake up and remember that Jason said something after the hug; that I must find some compassion for myself.

14. The Assignment

His daughter needed help with her homework, and Alistair stepped up. Lucy had a meeting tonight, so even though history was usually her department, he was enthusiastic to have the chance. He enjoyed being so willing, so committed to making sure his kids were OK. They sat at the kitchen table and analyzed the problem.

"I have to write about the Holocaust," she whined. "I don't understand the questions. Well, I understand some of them. But I don't understand this one about 'why do I think Hitler targeted the Jews.' It doesn't say why in the book." She frowned at the textbook, willing it to reveal its secrets.

"Well... if the question says 'why do you think,' it calls for your opinion, not just some answer given in the book anyway. Your opinion informed by the knowledge you've gathered in the book and at school. Did Miss Winters say anything about why the Jews were persecuted by the Nazis in class?"

"No, not really, it just seems really mean," said Florrie, with 13-year-old despair at the inhumanity of man to his brother, cushioned by a charmed and nurtured life, a life that described mass murder as 'mean'. Florrie's strict moral code forbade even the squashing of an ant. The marching of millions of people to their deaths in gas chambers, Alistair reckoned, must seem like the darkest fantasy, a tale of horror and carnage entirely beyond her ability to grasp. It was, frankly, beyond his. He had a fleeting and deep understanding of the sacred importance of history.

"Well, sweetheart, it is hard to understand. But maybe you can give a general answer. Why do people hurt other people at all? Why do people have wars?"

"I don't know," said Florrie, annoyed at the question. "Because they're stupid?"

"There may be a bit of stupidity there indeed," said Alistair. He was warming to the task. His body language was all edge-of-the-seat and emphatic gesticulation. "But try to relate it to your own life experience. Have you ever been unkind to anyone? Or seen your teacher be unkind to any of her students?"

"I'm not *unkind*," said Florrie, vastly insulted.

"I know you're not, sweetie. But how about other people in your class? Or your teacher?"

Florrie seriously considered the question. "Well, Jimmy is pretty mean. He can't stand it if he's losing at football, so he says mean things to whoever scored a goal on him or whatever."

"And why do you think he does that?" asked Alistair, with muted expectation.

"I don't know. Because he's an idiot?" exclaimed Florrie, fed up with the task.

"Well, yes, as we said, there's probably a bit of thoughtlessness in play here. So people act stupidly. But why do they act stupidly? What do you think people who are hurting other people are feeling?"

"Um... angry?" ventured Florrie.

"Yes, yes. Anger. And why are they angry? Why do people get angry?"

"Um... because they're stupid?" tried Florrie. Stupidity seemed to be a partially right answer, anyway.

"Even smart people get angry," said Alistair, proud of his ability to counter Florrie's obstinacy. "Why does anyone get angry? Why do you get angry if Max starts playing with your things?"

"Because they're mine, and he might mess them up," said Florrie, indignant at the very idea of Max messing with her stuff.

"Well... " continued Alistair, patience coming more easily than it usually did. "Can you apply your own experience to Hitler?"

There was a pause as Florrie stared blankly at her dad. Then abruptly she stated: "Hitler was afraid the Jews were going to mess up his stuff."

"Yes! Yes, exactly. Well done. You might want to put it a different way in your answer. But there's something else in what you said. Just how you said it. What did you just say just now?"

Florrie, somewhat disappointed that this wasn't the end of it, repeated "Hitler was afraid... "

"That's it." Alistair felt like he was channeling Lucy and her 12-step-program Spiritual Toolkit. It felt great; he felt wise beyond himself, as if all the wisdom of the world was available to him if he was sufficiently motivated. "Hitler was afraid. There is no anger, and violence, without fear. Hitler was actually afraid of the Jews. He thought they had too much power, too much economic power mainly. He was afraid the Jews were going to take away the Germans' stuff. He thought they already had, really, so he wanted to take it back. He thought the Germans were so great that they should rule Europe, if not the world. So he invaded all those other countries. He was afraid the Germans weren't going to get the power they deserved, and the territory. And to get the Germans to think the same way, he got supporters, and they told everyone a lot of stories about why Jews were so horrible, called them dirty, and made a big deal about their different religion, and pretty much made them a group that seemed less than human, so the Germans wouldn't mind if he treated them badly. He took away their homes, made them live in concentration camps, and killed them. Plus Hitler was crazy. He really believed all the nonsense he said. In fact some of the people closest to him tried to have him killed in the end, because he was so obviously nuts." Alistair took a breath. Florrie was listening, in the detached way of the privileged and protected, while Daddy described monstrous humanity in gentle and age appropriate vocabulary. "Do you think you have enough for an answer?"

"Yes Daddy," said Florrie, with the deeply grateful tones of a child well-versed in parent handling. "Thank you so much. I can write a good answer now."

He rose, kissed her head, and left the kitchen, very pleased with himself. Hitler was on his mind. Hitler and his charismatic ramblings, disturbing charm and ability to persuade an entire people to sanction evil. His rise on the tide of Germany's shame and defeat. The black and white footage that one saw occasionally of him wowing the crowds played in his mind, the man speaking with unnatural passion, crossing his arms before his chest in grandiose fervor; even the old tapes, seen with 20-20 hindsight of the horrors that ensued, compelled uninterrupted viewing. From those flat, grainy images still emanated some dangerously mesmerizing lunatic energy.

Alistair flopped onto the sofa and turned on the news, which led off with two British soldiers killed in Afghanistan. He felt no despair that the world hadn't changed, or learned the lessons of history . He felt simply wonderful. He snoozed a bit. There was faint clattering in the kitchen as Florrie put away her books. Languidly he reached for the guru book and opened it at random.

'It's looking at something and without any doubt being that thing. It's being somewhere and there are no boundaries between you and where you are, or where you seem to be. It's an

awareness that what seems to have happened is only memory happening right now, and the next thing that happens doesn't really happen in the future, it is always now. There is only this, and I am that, but there is no separation. It's not necessary to label it; it's just a shift in how everything is seen. It's seen that suffering is as much a gift as joy, for it is part of everything, and you are everything, so everything is available. It's seen that there is no right or wrong, just existence; and it's seen that no right and no wrong doesn't mean anarchy, they don't mean anything, it all goes along just as it always has, because there is nothing wrong with what seems to happen, it was just the dreamer that thought there was. Wholeness and completeness and unconditional love, it's right under the dreamer's nose, expressed in absolutely everything, every bird call, every thought, every feeling, every disaster, every violent urge. It couldn't be more obvious; it is this. It loops round, or seems to, back to everything just exactly as it is.

Oneness has no interest in whether the dreamer renounces anything, or lets go of his ego, or restrains himself; ego is oneness, ego-ing. The assertion of a "right" way and a "wrong" way is surely proof that duality is still being dreamed, that the mind is still wrestling with the simultaneous coexistence of mutually exclusive polarities, which can never be resolved by the mind, the tool of duality. The really comically funny thing is, that, of course, everybody is doing just exactly as they must, and there is nothing wrong or right about the debate. It all unfolds, or seems to, as it should.'

I have no idea, thought Alistair, what the fuck this book is trying to say.

15. The Risk

I have friends now in the loony bin. We chew over our damage and healing mostly in the cafeteria, along with the comfort food. Chase, an old rehab buddy, whose life is paralleling mine as he finds himself back again with depression, accuses me of falling in love with my psychiatrist. I protest. Later, cross-legged on the bed, I poke the bundle of feelings reserved for Jason. They unravel to display gratitude, and worship. Not "in love" then, but a mirror; what care he feels and shows for me is what I must feel for myself; self-love, the Holy Grail of therapy. It all has something to do with practicing risky behavior. I imagine us in the everlasting therapeutic stance, and I tell him I love him. He smiles a small smile. He doesn't reply. It doesn't matter. And, as simply as that, I find out that I'm capable of unconditional love.

I place enormous importance on this. I text Jason with the news, riding on a brief state of bliss, free fall, risky; some all-enveloping flash that this is all there is, this love. Not a feeling, not a concept. Just what I am. I wander about my little loony-bin cell, a two-star hotel standard room, grinning, saying to myself, "I'm not broken. It's Healing Day. I'm not broken. Never broken."

Still being human (I'm checking all the time), in our next session I find I'm asking Jason how he feels about me.

"Now I'm going to do my psychiatrist thing and stall for time," he says, smirking nervously.

He tells me things I have trouble accepting. That he always liked me. That he asked after me, from patients he knew had been in rehab with me. He likes my style. He likes the whole Bohemian thingy; I remember I'm supposed to be an artist (another pretend job, a handy, flaky front for the randomness of active addiction).

"Why do you ask?" he finishes.

"Hmmm, um, I guess I'm just human, and want to be loved," I reply, embarrassed. "But also, I just need to have the courage to ask. And deal with whatever you say."

"Well done," says Jason absently.

"Well, just to get it over with, I love you," I say, blood roaring in the ears.

"Hmmm... OK, I'll have to admit, I've had loving feelings for you. Especially when you let go of all the feelings about Max." He looks at me.

"I could tell," I say.

We have one of those therapy silences. We make eye contact. His face relaxes quickly, and changes into what seems like a non-threatening leer. There is unmistakable, powerful sexual tension. I'm surprised. I raise my eyebrows at him.

"Well," he says.

"I'm glad that's over," I reply, after a pursed-lipped whooshing sigh. "Dare we try a hug?"

"I was just going to ask permission," he says as we rise from the chairs.

We hug chastely. As I traverse the hospital corridors, I feel the sexiest woman alive. I pull out my mobile and phone Alistair.

16. The Flashback

Sitting cross-legged on the bed again, scribbling madly in my diary, I pour out the details of my last big drink, 15 years ago, before the relapsing, when I first got sober. It was characterized by leaving my husband, living with my parents, and binging several days at a time. I would crash with whomever would buy me a drink, and usually sleep with him. I had no currency but my cunt. My morals were nothing but violated. I stare at the diary, re-reading the vitriol that I still reserve entirely for myself. "I was a slut, and never once thought of anyone but myself," I read, and huge dismay at the self-loathing I still harbor engulfs me. Do I *still* hate myself so much? I feel the utter disdain, the lack of forgiveness I have for Lucy, the dirty, filthy stinking, whoring, child-abusing drunk.

Half an hour later I sit with Jason and tell him how surprised I am at how much, how incredibly much, I still hate myself.

"There's nothing wrong with you," he says. "There never has been. Addicts do whatever they have to do to stay in active addiction." He pauses. "You're quite a wonderful person," he says, "so creative, an unusual specimen for a suburban mum. Not exactly your everyday figure in the schoolyard."

He chuckles. Every little bit of praise, faint or sexually overt, however inappropriate it may be (and I never feel it is even slightly inappropriate), feeds my starved little ego.

Then WHAMMO! I am in a blue basement, a lurid blue mini-lampshade on a shelf with a matching blue throw on the armchair; the most hateful shade of turquoise, a color I cannot abide. There is a big man on top of me. No, no, I scream in my head. He fumbles with his dick, shoves my legs further apart with his knees, pins me down with his shoulders and rams it into me with all his strength. "Stop, please," I gasp, utterly ineffectual, and there is no lubrication to speak of so it begins to burn, to really hurt. He lunges into me as far as he can go; he is too big for me, and the knocking on my cervix is agony. I go silent and it is hell, it goes on and on, the pain is unbelievable, I long for it to end. At last he's finished. He rolls off. He smells lovely, of cocoa butter, which is never again for me the smell of beach and sun and sand.

I am back in Jason's office. He is kneeling beside me, holding me. "You're safe, you're here, you're safe," he says.

Raped all those years ago, at the end of my drinking, a crime born of the willingness I had to do anything, to go anywhere with anyone who would buy me a drink.

17. The Airport

"You're far from home," said the eldest soldier, a sweet-faced man of about forty. "Can we get you off this road?

"Nice hat," said a youngster in the back and they laughed, warily rather than merrily. Wariness informed their actions, Jason noted, as he slipped into the passenger side of the front. The soldier he had displaced slid in beside him. He was nicely squashed in the middle.

"What's your story? It's not the best place in the world to be wandering on the road," said the officer driving. Jason encapsulated his story, stressing the unlikelihood of the Taliban pursuing him.

"It's just possible," said the officer, "but not so much in Pakistan. Not even here so close to the border. They're not meant to be in that village. In fact, we're not meant to be here, either. We're stationed in Afghanistan. US military personnel are not welcome in Pakistan. We're looking for a stray buddy." All the soldiers, four of them, looked uneasy. Awol? Jason wondered.

"I'm not here, either," said Jason.

"Absolutely. You're not here and neither are we," said the officer.

Jason felt new love for the wanton global self-interest of

Americans as they roared, brazenly, smack in the middle of the road, to the airport.

The soldiers dropped him off as close as they could, and gave him some water and what looked like granola bars. They couldn't stop joshing, they were a laugh a minute, every statement was joke fodder. His makeshift turban was the source of much merriment. His adventure running from the unseen Taliban was met with more skepticism and a load of jokes about smelling them if not seeing them, and the gullibility of tourists, and old British soldiers craving excitement. He let it slip he was a psychiatrist, and his naiveté was even further lampooned; the soldiers wanted to know how crazy *they* were, fighting these ghosts with real artillery.

His Englishness was plundered too as the Americans made fun of the British soldiers' renowned politeness to the natives, and how they'd shake hands even when the hand had just been blown off. There was no hysteria in their laughter. Jason realized they considered themselves on a proper break on their nefarious errand in Pakistan, and they were using every moment to release as much dopamine into their frazzled nervous systems as possible. He felt, by the end of the journey, a bit battered, but privileged to have been a tool for their respite.

"Whatever you do, don't put that turban on again, they'll shoot on sight," said the soldier who disembarked to let Jason clamber out of the Humvee, to a chorus of nervous laughter. However, the boys in the back kept waving goodbye until they were out of sight, like small children leaving their summer sojourn at Grandma's farm. Plaintive waving, not wanting the moment to end.

Now the airport was defeating him. There didn't seem to be any way to get back to leafy Hampstead that didn't cost a thousand pounds.

Somehow, he had left his wallet at the hotel, with his money, most of his cards and his phone. All he had was his non-exchangeable ticket and one emergency credit card, tucked in the secret pocket of his rucksack.

He found his airline counter and, very much himself again, poured his considerable charm onto the ticket agent, to no avail. His return ticket was for a week hence and he apparently needed to leave today. He was reduced to lying; his daughter had developed a grave virus and had been suddenly admitted to hospital; he hoped his fantasy didn't somehow conjure a malevolent energy, and he would arrive to find his daughter actually in hospital, stricken down by the sins of the father. He couldn't very well tell the agent he was being chased by some phantom Taliban contingent, and had committed to playing out the Colonel's fantasy, which had generated an ill momentum of its own. He was back in the warm and fuzzy world of convenience and infrastructure; he could easily wave his one credit card at the problem, shell out the extra money, and be on a flight that afternoon. But he didn't want to. What might break his unreasonable resolve was the need for civilization in the form of a shower and a change of clothes.

"I'm so sorry, sir, but the ticket you have purchased simply does not allow you to exchange it," said the nice but bureaucratically robotic agent; a lady liberated by work, Westernized in her makeup choices, hair only loosely covered by a no-nonsense scarf. It was Pakistan, but even Partition and Islam couldn't dampen the genetic Indian tendency to stick by the rules no matter what. To fill in every form that could be filled, to dot every T, to cross every I, and then to go back and methodically correct any errors.

Jason felt both ashamed and empowered by his bigotry.

"Well, perhaps you could help me in another way," he wheedled, hoping to wow her with his humility, vulnerability and resonant, posh tones. "I'd love a shower. Is there anywhere in the airport I can get one?"

In her eyes there flickered a subtle change from complete obstinacy to possible mercy. Great, he thought, my body odor may save the day.

"Are you a member of Virgin Flying Club or British Airways Oneworld?" she asked, looking hopeful.

"Well, as a doctor, I'm not really required to travel like some professionals," he said, shamelessly playing the Doctor card, "But I seem to recall using the BA lounges when I traveled pretty frequently in the early 90's." He smiled his warmest smile, and allowed, for the first time on this trip, his sexual charisma to flow. It was powerful, and was sometimes a problem with his patients, both female and male, although often a therapeutic spotlight. Again, he felt empowered, for she responded; she smiled back, and looked up at him from beneath her eyelashes; in a moment, if not restricted by the mores of her culture and her job, she would be giggling. Her hands went clacketty clack on the keyboard, an expert in finding the loophole that would give some lucky passenger the Right to Supersede the Rules. She found the right screen with the right code, produced the right mini-form from the right cubbyhole, wrote the right phrase on it, and signed the right initials.

"Just show them this form and your return ticket at the BA executive lounge," she said, officious but softer. "You may use all the amenities there, including the shower. And I hope your journey continues more smoothly."

"So do I," he answered, but not antagonistically. There was something in her tone that suggested that, although she couldn't help him further, she hoped someone would.

Freshly showered and relaxed by a precious cup of Traditional English tea provided by the lounge and its obsequious attendants, he emerged and prowled the airport, half expecting to be paged or cornered or pistol whipped; the ghosts of the pursuing Taliban were still with him. Mostly he was determined to fly home as soon as possible on the ticket he had purchased for next week. He found a courtesy phone and called the Virgin ticket line, and met with much the same bureaucracy. He went to the airport authorities, who held up their hands in complete defeat at the power of his non-exchangeable ticket. He went back to the ticket counter, where a young man now spouted the universal concern for following rules. He was about to admit defeat and pay up, unable to dispel his fear of being hunted and his need to get out NOW. As he sat surrendering mentally on the hard chairs near the ticket counter, a man sat next to him and called him by name.

"Jason?" he said. It was Theodore Lipton, one of his most outstanding successes as a psychiatrist. A man in hellish despair for years, who, with Jason's patient and unswerving acceptance, and his own complete willingness to take risks, had recovered from his suicidal depression to become a renowned life coach and international speaker. He wrote books along the *You Are What You Think You Are* lines. Jason had always felt Theodore had taken the ball, ran with it, and disappeared into some world of complete confidence and joy that Jason couldn't completely comprehend. However, he wished him well there on Planet Motivation. He was, in fact, delighted to see him now.

"Theo! I certainly didn't expect to see you here." Jason had a brief surge of fear that Theo had stalked him there, but dismissed that as caution rather than grandiosity. Anyway, a stalker might be good company. At least he could be assured of acceptance. Even though, with each defeat, he felt more a part of this airport and its red tape and its passing ragtag humanity than alien from it.

"Dr. Jameson, it's really good to see you. What brings you here?"

"Visiting family," replied Jason, keeping his biographical information vague from sheer habit. "I'm trying to exchange my ticket to get out of here, but that doesn't seem possible. They're determined to get me to pay for another ticket. They're keeping me very busy jumping through hoops."

"Trying to get home," said Theo, wisely. "Like Dorothy."

"This isn't much like Oz," said Jason. "The natives are taller." They laughed. "And Glinda the good Witch would be

54

subject to all the worst punishments of Sharia," added Jason, and they laughed more. Jason had that feeling of being not so much himself. He was going with the flow; in fact, he was the flow. Theodore, he thought, would approve. It sounded like one of his pieces of wisdom, contained in tomes with names like *You Have Everything You Need*, £24.95 from Amazon.co.uk.

"So you're trying for the 5:45 to Heathrow," said Theo. "Maybe I can help."

"Please feel free to try," said Jason, without much real hope. But hope, he mused, is overrated.

Theo took Jason's ticket and passport to the counter. In a few minutes he rejoined Jason, with some new paperwork. "You'll be joining me on the 5:45," announced Theo, not at all smugly.

"How did you manage?" asked Jason, not at all surprised.

"Well, they obviously didn't appreciate what an important man you are, and how vital your work is in the UK," he said. "Also, I'm pretty shaky, and need my therapist with me when I fly."

"*You* obviously have everything you need, Theo," said Jason, amused.

"As do we all. And you taught me that," said Theo.

Jason bent to the forms, a snatch of a remembered poem gently playing on a loop in his mind.

> Dorothy crashed into a witch
> The victim of a windy glitch.
> She gathered friends, the land to roam,
> But never left her un-lost home.

19. The Rapist

Before I next see Jason, I tell Alistair about my memory. He is understanding, and I can tell it's not quite the shock it could be since it happened 15 years ago. The PTSD is so vivid and sudden that I only venture out of my room to eat. I write reams in the diary, each word bloated with consternation at the fact I still want to kill myself. What a piece of shit I am. I remember more, notably that after I left the rapist's apartment in his mum's basement, I ran in front of a bus. Prosaically, the bus screeched to a halt a couple of meters clear and the driver vented his adrenaline-fuelled shock by calling me a stupid bitch. I silently agreed and scuttled away.

I finally sit across from Jason and tell him that the first session of sexual intercourse with my rapist had been consensual. The whole thing would never hold up in court.

"You were fucked," says Jason, surprising me with the profanity, "both literally and figuratively."

"OK," I agree.

A pause.

"I have a hard time letting go of the idea that it was my fault, and I deserved it," I continue. "I still want to kill myself. I could just do with a bottle of vodka, about 300 pills and a locked attic."

"Tell me about the rape," he says. "Go through it. Let it play like a video in your head."

So I do, reliving the whole thing, complete with terror, disgust, and hatred. This time the hatred is shared between me and my rapist.

"He was a moron," I finish. "He was off his head as well. He actually didn't have a clue he was fucking someone who didn't want it. In fact, when I asked him for a drink in the morning, he actually seemed concerned. Like he'd seen morning drinkers before, and it was no good." I feel a bit sad for the clueless asshole, just for a moment. "I'm sure he had no idea he raped me. God I hate him, the brutal, stupid bastard. But I hate myself more for putting myself in that situation."

"Your feelings are changing," Jason notes.

"I hate the motherfucker," I say. "Christ, I had no idea I was even capable of hating someone besides me. I'd happily kill him. Well, maybe not. I'd happily cut off his dick."

"You're making progress," says Jason archly.

"It wasn't my fault. I don't believe I said that," say I, almost amused by my own change of heart. I remember a chat I had that morning with a fellow patient. We swapped post-traumatic flashback stories, marveled at how real, how sensory the memories were. Then he started crying, my fellow sufferer, and said he doesn't want to remember, because he's sure he hurt someone. "Perpetrators can have trauma too," I said wisely, spouting my new expertise obtained in an hour's surfing the Internet. The conversation ended at this point and I made my way to Jason's office, but now it carries on in my imagination. "Listen, I was raped," I imagine telling Possible Perpetrator, "and I forgive my rapist. If I can do that, you can forgive yourself for whatever it is."

"Oh my God," I say, back with Jason. "I know I just said I wanted to cut his dick off, but I forgive him. I actually forgive him, the cross-eyed, ugly stupid son-of-a-bitch."

"How extraordinary," says Jason.

20. The Zone

Alistair had almost forgotten why he ever went to that meeting with the enlightenment guru; something to do with understanding Lucy better. It was a noble motivation, born of love and concern, but he was beginning to think it unnecessary. He watched her cook in her immensely focused way and felt he knew her, that he *was* her obscurely. All the perversities that make up a human, all the lack of malice and malicious defensiveness, all the pulls and chops and changes that make someone who they are, he felt he couldn't possibly know more about another person. He knew her better than he knew himself, because with himself he hid things. With Lucy, it was all laid out for inspection; more importantly, he knew what she felt like, every inch of her body; and most importantly, he knew what her presence felt like. Anything worth knowing and feeling and perceiving, he already possessed the full package.

In fact, he wished he hadn't gone to see the guru. He found it all very alarming, and when he told her this, she said "Of course you do" very irritatingly. Lucy was a poem on legs, a sweet victim of life and the conqueror of his heart, and that's all he needed to know, or feel.

Nonetheless, he sat at the bleach-scrubbed kitchen table and pretended to read the guru's book, hoping Lucy would notice. He stared uncomprehendingly at a page:

'The whole "there is no one" thing seems a great, immutable block for a lot of individuals, and it isn't surprising. Golly, how we seem to need something to do. We are encouraged to take responsibility for our lives, to take back our power, and to make healthy choices; or else to let go of control, have faith, trust, and things go better for it. We are told we have so much wrong-thinking and it needs to be dissected and peeled back a bit at a time, and then, only then, will we see the Absolute or however we are referring to it today. Locked in that idea of a separate self, anything that is attempted to annihilate the self only reinforces the idea that it exists. Despite the favorite colors, personal struggles, singular personalities, overwhelming feelings, inextricable complexities and giant piles of undone life administration, despite poverty and injustice and casual homicide, despite joyous discovery and the pleasure of company, despite all those things on the evening news that scream and reinforce the notion we are separate individuals involved in a personal journey of survival and fulfillment, we are not. "Letting go and letting God" is a close second to immediate, complete, fulfilled existence, that is "always" and everything. This is free fall, this is what it is just as it is, and we are lived. Yet that includes the confusion and fear. That includes the despair and frustration. Ask any question, there is no answer; yet the answer is always embracing you. The play of life, it seems, has become enjoyable. There is no guarantee, but that is how it seems. It matters not what "you" "choose" to do; it will be the perfect choice.'

This made him angrier than ever, mostly at Lucy, who would know that any questioning of his personal volition would upset him beyond anything else. All the same, he knew what the guy was getting at. Maybe some other self-help book or well-paid therapist would put it as "being in the zone," when you're just being lived without thinking about it too much, and functioning at the top of your game. Some other part of the brain takes over, the intuitive part, and everything you've ever learned is perfectly synchronized and utilized. He supposed this guy, and Lucy, believed that that's always the case, you're always "in the zone" even when you're fucking up royally. Religious types would say we're divine puppets or suchlike. But Lu's lot seemed dangerous because they stopped taking the game seriously. They didn't try to fix what was wrong; in fact they emphasize, that nothing *is* wrong. And they implied that when you stopped fighting, "the zone" is all there is, and all there ever was, whether you're fighting it or not.

He flipped forward a few pages and read:

'Everything that seems to arise is seeking. Working, raising a family, going to church, attending satsangs, going to therapy, writing a musical, dating, getting married, donating to charity, volunteering for a worthy cause, breaking and entering to fund the heroin habit, drinking to oblivion, lashing out in anger, trying to be a better friend/spouse/parent, saving the planet, trying to scrape through the credit crunch, devoting all your time and energy to caring for an elderly parent, getting through the chemo, grieving for your lost child; it is all the same thing. There is some nebulous goal at the end of it: this life of mine will work, it will mean something, I will feel good about it, I will achieve it with some modicum of grace. Or it is all fueled by a sense of disappointment, unworthiness, and incompleteness; despair that the goal will never be met. This is the goal. The goal has been met, it is always being met. Whatever the story seems to be, however difficult life's circumstances, or blessed, the goal is met. This is the goal. This is unconditional love, being cancer or being a tragic accident or being charismatic leadership or being that tree over there, or your child, or the chair, or your best friend, or you. Even that sense of incompleteness is paradoxically immaculate wholeness. And it is glaringly,

overwhelmingly obvious, but not to the dreamer in the dream of being a separate individual. This is God, if you want to use that label. Everything is God, everything is love, everything is, and in existing, has met the goal. And if this is seen, the only thing that is missing is what seeks. It all seems to go on much as before, but perhaps without the sense of loss. Rejoicing is not the goal, but freedom seems to bring with it – sometimes "quickly", sometimes "slowly" – a lot of joy. Joy even in sorrow, for sorrow is. Joy in struggle, joy in more traditionally joyful things as well. But even the peace of sitting in a meadow or seeing your child asleep, safe and sound, is not the goal. It is all the goal. You've done it already, you are always doing it. This is it.'

Well, he thought. I might actually agree.

Door clicks and slams announced Max and Florrie's return from school. "Hi Mummy, hi Daddy," they chorused, swooping into the kitchen, smelling of the outdoors and pre-pubescent sweat, kissing each of their parents in turn.

21. The Connection

So what defines me now? The demons are faced, the abusers forgiven. The self, accepted. Mental Health achieved. Who am I? Why aren't I happy?

Is happiness even the goal?

It's been a couple of months since the breakthrough, the forgiveness. And this is depression, without the anesthetic. Ironing, back home, coping well, being responsible – Alistair is deliriously happy, if that's his goal then he's there – I steam a cuff and think: I will always feel like this. This is life. It's meaningless and pointless, and all this torturous work has been for nothing. Unaddled by mind-altering substances, I'm free to experience my Existential Crisis. Fucking good for me.

Why am I not unselfish? Why the still near-constant self-regard? Why am I not possessed of an organic altruism, keen to make the best of my life, filled with that unconditional love I feel so keenly around Jason? Why do I not float on a cloud of fulfillment, devoted to each task, doing whatever the moment gives me to the best of my abilities, all of it flowing freely from my inmost self, my divine source, unencumbered by the resistance born of fear? Now that all the demons are exorcised, that all the facets of my personality and their purposes are known and integrated into this miraculous bundle of Me, why don't I walk around a realized, whole and complete self, just happy being here? Just happy. Will I ever be happy?

Is happiness the goal?

Maybe, as they reiterate ad nauseam in the 12-step rooms, acceptance is the goal. Just bearing whatever the feelings, thoughts, and circumstances are at any given time. Well, if that's the case, the goal is met. This is bearable. It's no longer torturous. It sucks, but it's bearable. Questioning the nature of existence in the mire of depression is not what I expected the outcome of facing my life with courage to have been, but I accept it.

"I was standing outside smoking," I say to Jason at the next session. I am nervous around him, I want to be well for him. Even such people-pleasing, a step backward by any measure – recovery from addiction, mental health, personal expectations – is accepted. "I suddenly had this vision of my insides, my psyche of whatever, and at the core was a little baby, sort of deformed and twisted. And I thought, maybe I'll never be well. Maybe I'll never be whole, maybe I'm too damaged. And it was OK. I sort of embraced the weird baby."

"You *are* whole," replies Jason simply.

"I believe you," I say. "I just can't see it." Very abruptly, I start to cry. Crying is still not a regular occurrence for me, and when it comes, pressure escapes like a feral cat from a shed. "I want to kill myself again," I admit. "I can't believe I still do. I want my suffering to end, I guess." My words are garbled by the ahuh, ahuh, aheh of the sobs. "But I think now that I don't really want to. That I fear life, not death. Wanting to kill myself is just hiding my love of life. My fear of life is my love of life. I'm afraid of getting it all wrong again." Ahuh, ahuh, aheh, tapering off now. "I don't know. I hear the in-laws talking about their dying friends and I guess I fear pain, infirmity, all that stuff. But I don't fear death, probably because I think of it as some kind of release." I grab a tissue from our little round barrier table and give an almighty snorking blow. And another – it is a very wet cry. We both appreciate the comedy, smirking at the lengthy nose-blow, and move on. "And I don't really want release. I'm all confused. It's like I've been given the most precious gift in the history of the Universe, and I still think something's missing."

Another pause, famous now. I look up, and Jason is bent forward, his face supported by his hands tripod style. The effect is fetching. He sits forward, and his face is aglow. The energy in the room seems golden.

"Lucy, sometimes your stuff brings up things of my own," he says, enthusiastically.

"That's pretty obvious," I state.

He throws his head back and chuckles; the effect is fetching. "That's pretty obvious," he repeats. "You know," he continues, "one never knows where therapy is going. I never suspected this would go so deep. You never know when the issues will be so similar." He is open, a thousand times less guarded than usual. "I have the same fears. In fact, this last weekend, I had to face my fear of death. I go to a spiritual teacher. He said to me, 'Yes Jason, you, too, are going to die,' and it was very, very powerful." He smiles a charismatic smile. "Every once in awhile, it's pretty rare," he says, and I hardly dare to hope what might come next, "there's a real connection." He beams at me, sitting back in the comfy chair.

"Thanks, Jason." I can't think of anything else to say for the reeling. Laid bare, under a layer of dread and a layer of hope, was a sweet little layer of vulnerability. For me, and so it would seem, for him too.

22. The History Lesson

It was strange, thought Jason, traveling through a bit of Pakistan and encountering both such civilization and such poverty, so many moderate beliefs and so much extreme behavior. It seemed as if ordinary citizens just wanted to carry on with mundane life but were pulled in ten directions by the psychotic people who tried to lead them. If the tribal warlords weren't raping their daughters and stealing their farms, the fundamentalists were promising to protect them; but if only they threw away their beautiful, Sufi-informed, moderate Islam and replaced it with some madness where women were reviled and men were constrained by absurdly barbaric rules. If the national government weren't lining the pockets of every crackpot group or nation that supported their continued power, they were parading leader after leader who, in the end, had no power compared to the military. Madrassas thrived, many of them teaching nothing but narrow-mindedness and fear, because the government let every broad-minded institution of learning rot. Jason had heard so many stories of lives lost, unvalued and disdained, for the betterment of the power-hungry or the madmen; or for the fear the Army had of the idea it wasn't supreme and might not deserve its absolute power.

Jinnah's vision of a secular haven for Muslims had turned into a factionalized, oppressed nation, vulnerable to anyone who would promise relief. The Islamisation of Pakistan must surely be around the corner. Jinnah must have had qualms as he witnessed the carnage that ensued as so many people were uprooted and displaced. The Colonel's story of the boy with bloody feet was probably one of the sweeter, nicer stories about Partition, the stories of mass murder and mob mentality too horrible to contemplate.

An academic from Karachi, Pervez, was seated next to him on the plane, happy to be finally escaping to London. Jason listened to his description of a country falling to pieces and felt no despair, just great peace. It wasn't *his* peace. Jason told him about his Taliban pursuers, and Pervez seemed to think that in all likelihood they weren't ghosts, but men who had heard of his infidel presence in a Muslim home and of his British nationality, and were probably hunting him as a suspected American spy. But he'd realized too that somehow, those energies must be played out. Jason wondered at the suffering of his patients, middle-class Londoners mostly, whose lives didn't involve having their daughters raped for intimidation, who weren't subject to military rule or fundamentalist demands that their lifestyle change beyond all recognition; the possibility that any stability they had ever known could disappear at any time was, for Londoners, unlikely. Yet their suffering was as real and intense as if they had those basic survival stresses. Life is everything, everywhere; people use whatever they have at hand.

Pervez, after his long discourse on the history of Pakistan, now slumped asleep beside him. Theodore caught his eye across the aisle, smiled and waved; Jason waved back, feeling slightly ridiculous, and noted that Theo seemed in that moment not so much a renowned lifestyle guru but a small, happy child. Jason felt glad that he, Theo's savior, had been delivered to Theo for him to rescue, a full circle, and proof that Jason was just a man. He never really rescued anyone. They were all perfect and whole, his patients; they just needed help to see it. Maybe just some validation, or perhaps a little readjustment of their brain chemistry accompanied by his acceptance and their courage. He joined Pervez in sleep and once the dreams that fizzed from his hyper-stimulated neurons had faded away, Jason was no more, and Jason, sleeping deeply, wasn't there to care.

23. The Vision

It's incredible, how good therapy can work, or deep engage-ment with anyone, I suppose. Without the social mask, but with agreed boundaries. I am back in the 12-step rooms where I get therapy for my therapy.

"You've fallen in love with your therapist," says Andrea knowingly. She is a veteran of 10-year-long therapy, and knows her business.

"There's love *in* the therapy," I subtly amend, "but if he didn't love me, I'd never believe I was worthwhile." This is something obvious I don't realize until I say it.

"Does it interfere with your marriage?" asks Charles, always good for a pertinent question. He reeks of long-term so-briety; it smells like tea and antiseptic. Acceptance is his motto.

"It enhances it," I reply, slightly defensive. "It's never been better with Alistair. Whatever I feel for Jason spreads to him, but with Alistair, it's backed up with an actual grown-up re-lationship. We've been together for 20 years, you know." Yet another truth I stumble upon not knowing I know it.

At home, I embrace my children as they greet me at the door, and it occurs to me I've never held them. I never com-pletely felt that sweet and raw presence. At some point, the wall fell down.

Preparing dinner, bangers and mash, I peel potatoes. Each sliver of skin falls into the sink. There is only potato peeling. Unexpectedly, I'm on a mountaintop. In the valley below, the scenes of my life play out, all the disappointing, wasted, brutal, cruel vignettes; and there is nothing wrong. There is nothing wrong with any of it. It happened.

There is, I realize at last, nothing wrong with *me*.

"And all those things that happened, Jason," I say to him the next day, "all that pain and abuse, endangering Max, being raped, all of it, it seems... it seems like some kind of huge gift." That may change, my caveat-laden mind reminds me; enjoy it while you can.

"What's happening to you," said Jason thoughtfully, "although I wouldn't call it rare... it's amazing. I'm delighted." He looks delighted. I notice his overstuffed brown leather chair, and the desk to the right, a very traditional Chairman of the Board piece with dark wood and a posh blotter; statuettes of Freud and Beethoven adorn the corners. There is a blue carpet with a tasteful diamond pattern, and a minimalist red and green blobby abstract painting on the wall to the left.

I'd never noticed any of it before.

24. The Subtle Change

The greatest saint, whose life we revere, whose selfless-ness we admire, whose tirelessness in helping others we envy: that life does not compare to the small triumphs of the victim redeemed. Lucy did nothing much differently, thought Alistair. The structure of her life, of the life of their family, remained stable. All the duties, chores and mundane tasks that make up being a stay-at-home mum and creative person were much the same; they had morphed as the children grew older, and Lucy certainly didn't need to use any of her creative energy to obtain her pills secretly and hide her pill-taking, but that energy simply manifested in a diary, a crocheted sweater, a neater house, and more time spent helping the kids with their emotional needs. This was a particular talent of hers, informed by the wisdom of 12-step programs and the past year of therapy.

No, thought Alistair, not much had changed. Their sex life was livelier and more frequent, but he didn't like to dwell on that too much, as he suspected it had to do with some spark between Lucy and her therapist. Yet indescribably, *everything* had changed. Whatever Lucy did, although the tasks remained the same, wasn't underpinned by some nebulous despair. Although not a picture of serenity by any means, she was confident in her anger, compassionate with her fear. And that's why Alistair picked up the dratted book again, and read, and tried to understand the errant nonsense within it. This business of not taking life seriously, yet doing it all with much muted passion and wry wisdom – well, he had to very grudgingly admit, there was probably something to it. He knew that her therapist had been instrumental in letting this happen, but that he wasn't the be-all and end-all of Lucy's redemption. Something had happened, some change of perception, and he wanted to know more. So he opened the book, reluctantly, and read.

'There is such discomfort in living in separation. All that we label "trouble" or "cruelty" stems from it. Adulterers being stoned to death by the Taliban are the victims of such extreme separation that not only is God a separate entity, that entity is cruelly judgmental and ruthlessly sadistic. God becomes a personification of fear in a land that is continually violated by invaders and torn by civil unrest, where there is no sense of safety, and where the fundamentals of life are constantly threatened. The Taliban may be cruel, but their existence is hardly a mystery. Separate countries war with each other, defending their piece of land, or perhaps grabbing some more land, the divisions stoked by the promise of safety and the egotistical building up of each nation as "good" and the other as "bad". The mind loves a story, and war stories are popular. We sit with suspicion always, see others who merely look somewhat different or speak a bit differently as so alien that they are mainly a threat, and rarely a breath of fresh air. We dislike differences, and comfort ourselves by pointing these differences out and using them to widen the chasm between "us" and the chimerical "them". Our own children's task and duty is to become more separate, and hopefully to evolve into the most unique and different individual that ever was, with as little resemblance to the parents as possible. This kind of separation is the burden of each small piece of humanity, and is, in fact, labeled "mental health". We seem like islands, alone

and isolated, apart with our little thoughts and overwhelming feelings; no one is like us, and no one could ever understand. We are at war with the world, and either try to get to know it, understand it and control it, or set up a fortress against it, engaging with it as little as we can get away with. Yet there is nothing wrong with any of this. Duality is as it must be, it is life looking at itself, but that doesn't mean it's not oneness. We are each other no matter what the color or flavor of that seems to be. Perhaps when this is recognized there will be less apparent cruelty born of fear, perhaps there will be more compassion, and more compassionate acts. But there is always balance, no matter how dismaying the extremes are. The balance may be more centered, but there is no guarantee. The stories may abound but this is wonderment, here it is, it never left, it is nowhere to be found; this is it.'

Alistair took the book, aimed, and flung it with all his might at the doorway leading to the dining room. Later, Lucy picked up pieces of the jigsaw that the book had scattered into each corner of the room. What on Earth have the kids been up to now, she thought.

25. The Argument

"I'm sorry," I say to Alistair helplessly. "I'm just low. I can't help it. I just am. I wish I wasn't." Wishing I wasn't isn't strictly true. But I know it's what he wants.

Alistair is a picture. He enthuses, he does things, lot of things; he's nearly always busy. His black Italian begotten hair is unruly and gorgeous, although he finds taming it a trial. He has a little middle-aged spread which I love. His face is so easy on the eye, not classically handsome but perfectly arranged. It is the face I've seen nearly every day for 20 years. Every time I look at him, he looks brand new.

Alistair is angry. I hate his anger, or anyone's somehow, and although childhood hasn't come into the therapy too much, as a child I learned to cope with anger by avoiding it, ameliorating it, making no fuss, being no trouble. Now, it's not so threatening.

"I've been very patient with you," he says. "It's been a year now. When is this all going to end? When do I get you back?"

"Maybe you've never had me. This is definitely some new, improved version." Calm words mean nothing to him now. He is up and pacing.

"New and improved? Maybe for a while. But I'm picking

73

up your slack again. You're not capable anymore. This is your family I'm taking about. You need to do the best job possible." He pauses, facing me, seeing how the words land.

Anger is conveniently replacing sorrow for me.

"Well Christ, excuse me. I didn't know you were rating my performance as a wife and mother and shitworker. Is that what counts? How well I make the kid's lunches? How caught up I am on the ironing? I've been through absolute hell this last year. I'm sorry I'm not up to standard! This is my best, just for now, Alistair. It's bound to get better; I can't make myself not feel sad. I can't help it." Anger was quick-stepping back into sorrow.

"I think you can," he retorts. "I think you're wallowing. In fact, I think you're just staying stuck so you have an ex-cuse to see your precious Jason. What is he to you, anyway?"

"What is he? He's my shrink. He's helped me beyond anything I ever could have hoped for. "Jesus," I fume, "what kind of perfection are you expecting? What do you want from me?"

"I want," and he appears to consider it, "I want us to be enough for you."

"So I'm not allowed to have a life? To try and get well?" I ask, whining a bit.

"This *is* your life. Your family. This should be enough. It's no joke, raising kids. They need you. I need you. Jason doesn't need you, we do."

"Why are you dragging him into it?" I yell. "He's had nothing but a positive effect on this family. It's better, surely to have me limping along a bit instead of dead?"

"There's no need to be dramatic." To align himself with his words, he calms visibly. "You're right, you're right," he says, having a mid-sentence change of heart, looking a little helpless. "I know you've had a hard year. I just miss you when you're like this. You were so well for awhile. I just want you back."

"I'm sorry," I repeat, also helpless. "I feel something is missing. I don't know what. I want to be here for you guys. I promise you it's my biggest priority, more than career or art or whatever the hell else it is I'm supposed to be about. But I can't just flick some switch. I feel... incomplete. I feel it's all so pointless. I'm sorry, I'm so sorry." Tears now, to which Alistair is unsympathetic.

"This *is* enough," he says, more wisely than either of us knows. "I'm tired of waiting for you." And having delivered this hard truth, he stalks out of the living room. I am left in despair, but it seems to slide away fairly quickly.

Our living room is Middle Eastern ethnic, like a genie vomited in an exploding carpet shop. I marvel at the samovars, the orange Turkish carpet – alive with flying diamonds – the busy but muted green and pink William Morris curtains, the big stuffed kilim-covered yellowy-orange cushions. I'd never taken in my own décor as a whole before. The little stick animals in the kilim pattern dance a bit.

26. The Brawl

Alistair sized up the competition. Lucy was apt to go on about Jason's age, his status as overweight, his gray hair. He knew now that this was just to throw him off the scent. There before him, in the comfy therapist's chair that mirrored his own, was one of those men who exuded musk, for whom when they walked into a room heads turned, and women adjusted their cleavage. Here was the Bill Clinton of the London psychiatric community. He might be trying to tone it down for Alistair's sake, but there was no hiding the sexual charisma. Alistair felt a twinge of aggression. He would have preferred a fight to this useless talking, an out-and-out brawl, where his fist could satisfyingly wipe the smugness off Jason's Oxbridge-educated face. But he was sure Lucy was his, although he wasn't allowed to say anything so direct and simple. She might be a mess, but she was *his* mess. Her pixie body, her pointy nose, her addiction, her damage – all his.

Somehow, he was going to exit this office the victor.

Alistair glanced up at a bobble-head Sigmund Freud, certificates on the wall, a snow globe with golden glitter that seemed to contain a little plastic shrink and a tiny plastic patient on a couch. Trophies that proclaimed Jason's status as beloved professional. Alistair wasn't intimidated.

He was going to win, even here in Jason's territory, the fight on Jason's turf, the terms Jason's.

"Well," said the doctor, and smiled. "You wanted to see me."

"Yes," said Alistair, tensed and ready, but reading as relaxed and vulnerable. "I just want some kind of update. If Lucy had cancer, the oncologist would tell me what was going on in the middle of chemo. So, I guess I just want to know what your opinion is of her progress. She comes to me with the most outrageous stories of her latest revelations. I guess she never remembered all these things that happened to her properly, not until now. So, I'm concerned. We have two children. Frankly, I want to know if she'll ever be up to being a good mother." There, thought Alistair, I sound like a real asshole. That should give him a lot to fuck up.

Jason triangled his hands thoughtfully, from the textbook of shrinky postures. "Well, Alistair, I think she's remarkable. I don't know if I've ever had a patient who works so hard. She's most definitely motivated to get better, to heal. Motivated by your children and by you."

Bullshit, thought Alistair. The reason he was here was his suspicion that Lucy was motivated by Jason, that she loved him. She wasn't making this stuff up exactly, but Alistair suspected she was dredging it up to give her plenty of reasons for seeing Jason a lot, and basking in his fucking healing presence.

"I hope so," was all he actually said.

"Are you uncomfortable with the intimacy of the relationship?" asked Jason. "Of another man being so close to your wife?" Jason's face was a mask, giving nothing away.

Oh no, thought Alistair, you're not going to get me by getting right to the point.

"Not if it's helping her," lied Alistair.

They lapsed into some specifics, particularly about the recollections that had the potential to be 'false recovered memories.' Alistair was honestly stunned; Jason, concerned.

Their motives met. The unspoken agenda wasn't just whether Jason might ever fuck his wife.

You're not sucking me in by reminding me we're both here for her best interests, thought Alistair. He decided to just get it over with.

"Is there any danger with you two? Should I be worried?" asked Alistair, all his resources to the fore.

"No," said Jason.

They shook hands, and Alistair left; reassured, but alert as always.

27. The Dream and the Memory

Jason's dreams returned over somewhere in Turkey. He dreamed of Pakistan; he was staying with a family. The son of the family had just showed him around the village, in some remote region, perhaps Kafiristan. There were inordinate amounts of tethered goats, children shouting at the sight of him, women in colorful scarves decorated with beads. There were dark skins with blue eyes. He sat in the boy's home, on the floor, in front of a sunken fire, and watched the smoke rise in a preternaturally straight column up to and out of an ancient hole in the ceiling. The boy's mother brought him a plate of food, goat meat and vegetables, and he and the father scooped it up in great mouthfuls with some torn bits of flat bread. "I'm a bit depressed," said the man. "Maybe you can help. I think it's that my she-goat has stopped laying. She's no longer a young goat. But the children love her, and I hate to slaughter her. Between you and me, we're eating her now." The meat, rather than becoming some horror or travesty, became tastier and more precious. "But what's really getting me down is that I had to kill my daughter last year." The man sighed a resigned sigh. "To save her from defilement by the warlords," he continued, matter-of-factly. "It was very hard on my wife."

"But I got her bed, it's much nicer," said the boy from the doorway.

"How dare you listen!" shouted the man, and threw his plate at the boy, who avoided it in a slow-motion dream-maneuver.

Pervez stirred, bumping Jason's arm, and Jason woke. He thought of telling the scholar of his dream. He went over it, keeping it fresh in his memory. He decided against sharing it. In fact, he was still sleepy, fairly exhausted by his adventure. He felt sure he had lost weight. He dozed, and remembered a conversation he'd had with a cranial neurosurgeon several weeks before his Big Trip to Pakistan on his Own to Visit his Sister.

It was at one of those insufferable convention-refurbished country house hotels, a coffee station every few meters, the original feel of the mansion pathetically preserved with screwed-on prints of hunting parties and gaudy hulking Victorian armoires in the corridors next to the lifts. They were in a function room named for some local minor Georgian celebrity, a former formal dining room now used for businessmen and professionals to congregate in a businesslike, professional manner. He was put between the neurosurgeon and a vaguely familiar shrink with whom he'd ghosted a dutiful research paper on relapse prevention when he was just setting up practice: so many, many years ago. His shrink colleague, aware of Jason's renown, was aloof and dismissive. The neurosurgeon, not being in any direct professional competition with Jason, and because all neurologists looked upon psychiatry as witch-doctory, was loquacious and enthusiastic.

"Tell me, Jameson," he drawled, "what do you think the brain is used for?" They'd already done the introductions (his companion's name was Dr. Arthur Morgan), a derisive review of the agenda, and the pouring of mineral water from the requisite up-market bottle placed before every second delegate.

"Um... " Jason was determined not to be caught out; it was undoubtedly a trick question: "... well, all the autonomic functions of the medulla oblongata. The processing of sensory input. The frontal lobe functions, personality, identity. Reflex reactions." He sighed. "But I know I'm being set up, so why don't you just give me the correct answer?"

Dr. Morgan was obviously pleased with Jason's response. "Ah, you're right. On all counts. But only because of my own surprise as I piece it all together," said Arthur, now smug, yet magnanimous. "The brain's function is almost wholly possessed of not just processing sensory input – which it obviously does as well – but with blocking it out. Filtering it, prioritizing it, keeping us from being bombarded so that we can truly focus on the task at hand. Whatever that may happen to be."

"What percentage? Do you know?" asked Jason, immediately relieved of the usual petty concerns that arose whenever he met with a group of colleagues. The task at hand was, for a change, interesting.

"Not know, not absolutely. But I'd hazard a guess at something high. Say 78% of brain function at any given time is comprised of blocking out anything judged to be extraneous."

"Who or what is judging?" asked Jason, spontaneously possessed by a good, obvious question.

"Well, that *is* the question, isn't it? Not by anything or anyone but the brain itself, perhaps before anything as specific and exotic as the personality becomes involved. It's fascinating. Endlessly fascinating." Arthur leaned back, a specific and exotic character, well pleased with the life he discerned.

Jason said, after a thoughtful pause, "Well, if the mind thinks it, it's a concept. It's a thought about reality, not reality. All the information the brain receives, and processes, even the sensory information about the solidity of this table – of you – of me – is a few firing neurons in the brain."

"That's so," replied Arthur, equally thoughtful. "That's why we went for the brain, my friend, although in different capacities. The brain is the real heart of the body, of the whole world. It *is* the whole world."

"I suppose you went for the actual organ, and I just cover the thoughts and feelings," mused Jason, feeling he understood why Arthur and his ilk thought psychiatry was away with the fairies.

"Ah. Don't suppose I dismiss psychiatry," said Dr. Morgan, reassuringly. "There is a lot of merit in relieving the suffering that the brain can inflict on itself, if there's no true organic interference. I'll take a nice, simple tumor any day, even if it turns out to be inoperable. *You* operate in the dark. In the dark, on the battlefield, in a tent, with a candle and a butter knife." Arthur smiled, again magnanimous.

"It certainly seems that way some days," Jason offered. "Most patients respond to nurture. To love, if you will. It seems to heal a lot of those damaging beliefs."

"In fact, I envy you your job," said Arthur. "You work with people. I work with tissue. Fascinating, endlessly stimulating tissue, but tissue all the same." Arthur didn't actually seem very envious, but Jason appreciated that he was breaking a cardinal rule: never give psychiatry validation.

"I started off in neurology, you know," said Jason. This was a tidbit he rarely shared. "I switched when I knew I enjoyed consulting with patients more than fiddling with their flesh."

Arthur laughed. "That's one of the best ones I've heard," he said. "I'm a flesh-fiddler. Oh yes, that just about covers it."

They chatted some about the worthy goal of the seminar – Brain Function, Behavior and Societal Conflict. It had brought the entire spectrum of professionals together who thought the other specialties were, at best, misguided. Politicians, therapists, brain researchers, shrinks and neurologists, all of who thought the others were wasting their time. Ironically, the societal conflict was mirrored in the seminar's delegates. Not surprisingly, few conclusions were reached.

Jason came back to full consciousness as the plane descended, noisily. He felt the emotions of his adventure and his memories, the anticipation of resuming his life with his family, and the excitement of resuming his practice, that procession of broken souls, needing mostly to be convinced of their own worth.

There were no lessons learned, no revelations, no new humility; no life-shattering changes had ensued as a result of what had passed in Pakistan. Yet he felt completely different; as if he were being constantly renewed in each moment. That was how it had always been, actually. That is, thought Jason, how it is.

28. The Longing

"Well, he's really a friend now; our families get together on weekends, for instance. Which puts a different spin on it all." Jason, at my request, is telling me all about his spiritual journey, specifically his teacher. "He's a funny little guy, short, bald, incredibly charismatic. I went to some talk he was giving, dragged there by a friend, and it just clicked." He looks at me, one eyebrow raised. "What do you know about nonduality, metaphysics, Advaita, enlightenment, Zen Buddhism, any of that kind of thing?" he askes.

"Um... nothing, really. Despite my arty-fartiness, I am *so* not new-agey or whatever. People start talking about chakras or start saying 'it's all about love' or any of that stuff, I roll my eyes and tune out." In fact, I don't realize I'm quite so skeptical until he brings it up.

"Yes. Well, as a doctor, you can imagine my attitude was a bit like yours, and then some. But I sat there, and what he said made sense. Or, it didn't actually make sense to me empirically, but it spoke to something I already knew. Something I already was. It's difficult to explain," he says apologetically. "It's what a lot of people call a spiritual awakening. It's the dropping away of the ego, I suppose. The goal of all seeking for the deepest answers. Have you any idea what I'm on about?" He leans forward, intrigued. I shake my head slowly, but I have already tuned out. My thoughts are elsewhere. How can I get by without this man? How can I just exist without the weekly punctuation of our visits? Who will I ever be able to talk to in such depth, and so freely? Without the problems of the past, I realize, my identity now revolves around him. And the therapy is bound to end. It has to end. Whatever possibilities there are between us have already been exhausted.

"No," I finally answer. "I really don't know what you're on about."

We finish up talking about Alistair and his former delight at my proficiency in life, now replaced by his disappointment at my depression. Nothing to do, we decide, but wait it out. We hug, and I leave the office with an almost unbearable longing. For something more with Jason, for a happy fulfilled family life, to be filled with the Holy Spirit, to get another film to work on, to eat, to have a drink, to have a piss. For whatever the fuck it is that's not here. It is, in fact, more a resonance of that yearning that makes it imperative that I drink, that I work, that I parent the kids within an inch of their lives, that I do everything in my power to please my husband, that I do anything at all – to excess. It is a resonance magnified and distilled to pure desire. And now, a drink won't cure it.

29. The Deal

There was so much work to be done, so many tasks and duties. The business of running and maintaining a family was an awesome one, and Lucy, Alistair observed, seemed to do it not as some serene and placid individual, possessed of some secret knowledge of the meaning and purpose of life, but as one who simply bore the tidal waves of emotion and conflicting needs. Before all this therapy and awakening crap, he thought, she had to run away from anything too intense; now, she just waited it out, as she got on with whatever it was she had to do.

And she was far more assertive with him. He would have thought he wouldn't like that. As it happened, it made him proud of her.

The task at hand was duvet stuffing and pillowcase changing, which he knew she loathed, or she used to anyway. He stepped up and started helping. She looked up at him, annoyed at her flow being interrupted, but accepting the help.

"Max seems to be nervous about his exams," he said, conversationally, although he was worried.

"Yes, but I guess he's learning to cope with his stress," she said. "There're no more tears at night. He seems to have gotten past the fear that he won't get into *any* school. Now he's just nervous about the exams themselves. That seems reasonable."

"There must be something more we can do to help him," said Alistair, Mr. Fixit. "What about that coaching stuff he got last season? About turning anxiety into excitement? That's it's all just energy, and it can be changed from one kind to another?"

"That's good stuff," said Lucy. "It almost sounds a little healy-feely. They say the same stuff to actors coping with stage fright. I guess it applies to any kind of performance."

"Well," said Alistair, managing self-parody while fighting with a duvet corner, "if it's new-agey, forget it. We should just tell him life is rough, and he has to go through hell for anything worth having."

"That'll work," replied Lucy, not rising to the bait. There was a smooth gentle humor between them. They gently smoothed the duvet cover, naturally in sync.

There were these mini-conversations four or five times a day. Monitoring the children's progress through life, debating the best ways to help them cope with challenges. So may tasks and duties, day in and day out.

Alistair went downstairs to collapse on his special armchair. The dreaded book was on the lamp table. It seemed to find him every time he chucked it away. Resigned, he thumbed it a bit and settled on a page where he spotted the word "cracked":

'There are no deals, in fact there is no one who can make a deal anyway; but the dreamer cannot make deals with oneness. When the dream of separation dissolves, as it can any "moment", there are no guarantees that everything gets "better". It may seem to unfold more efficiently, since there is not the extra added "me" trying to control and understand and make right choices and accept and reject and generally make a mess of it; but there is the same appearance of the usual mind/body organism, the same old human character, with all the same apparent

memories and conditioning, and things go on pretty much as they always did. When this is seen, it is also seen that that's all that ever happened anyway. Even in the many parables, the stories we tell and the stories we live, freedom is not always the fantastic thing it's cracked up to be. But to see this – that all there is, is this – is liberation. It is unlikely, in the story that seems to unfold "after" this is seen, that there is so much concern about getting everything right. There is no one to get it right. It is right. It is what it is. What is seen is that what happens is eternal and wondrous, and a fragile appearance, yet a fantastic and fascinating one. Perhaps it's likely that there's less despair, less hand-wringing, and less yearning for what is missing. There is nothing missing. The apparent reality, filled with politicians and hunger and suffering and joy and birth and charity, is a mere appearance, and is appearing as it must. No one owns it. There is no choice at any level. It is gloriously and divinely this.'

Max entered the living room, mock exam under his arm. Lucy followed, wearing a controlled expression of amusement.

"Mummy, Daddy, I have an idea," he said, full of enthusiasm. "If I get into all of the schools, can I have some kind of reward? Like an i-phone or a PlayStation? Because it would be a lot easier if I had some kind of... what's the word, Mum?"

"Incentive," Lucy monotoned.

"Yeah, incentive, incentive, I remembered it upstairs," said Max.

There was little stock an 11-year-old could put into the assured future, full of options, that an education was supposed to make possible. However, a new toy, secured in the short term, was powerful motivation. A negotiating session followed. Terms were agreed. In the end, a PSP was the prize on offer. Max trundled off, throwing "I'm going to do a practice exam now" over his shoulder.

He sat next to Florrie at the kitchen table, where she was having her computer time. Florrie MSN'd with her best friend as Max did his best with the odd and alien-looking patterns of a non-verbal reasoning test. Florrie laughed at a funny picture her friend had sent her, of a lemur looking at his crotch with the logo "OMG WTF" underneath. "Shhh," hissed Max, severely. Florrie rolled her eyes. They were cozy within their world, where they were very busy becoming the most unique and special individuals that have ever existed.

30. The Beginning of the End

I embrace Alistair in our kitchen. We're in a full body contact clinch. I can feel his fast-becoming-impassioned penis, and we collapse in lust. The kids are off to school, and thus free, he turns me around and we have the most delicious knee-trembler right there on the kitchen counter. We have always been sexually compatible, Alistair and I. Our relationship is simple. We're in it for the long haul.

I feel blessed and fortunate thinking about Alistair and our 20 years as I watch him gather up the tools of his business in the jungle. There is some heightened quality to it, blissful, unencumbered, to both the feeling of gratitude, and to Alistair's movements; familiar, yet new; he picks up his briefcase, he puts on his blazer. Déjà vu.

"Have a great day, my Love God," I tell him.

"I am not worthy of such a sex goddess," he replies, his mind obviously roving ahead to work. But that's what he does. It's fine.

I sit later with Jason, and am startled to realize the depression has lifted. I've done my time, for now.

"We have to start thinking about ending the therapy," he says. Frankly, I've been imagining this for ages. A little annoyed thought surfaces in my brain, like a tub-fart.

"I wanted to be the first to say it," I complain. "That way, *I'd* be dumping *you.*"

"It's not 'dumping' by any means," he starts, "it's part of the process... "

"SPARE ME THE SHRINK TALK," I yell. He is gratifyingly startled.

We sit in silence. Not one of those therapy pauses; not the classic silence of psychoanalysis, where the analysand fills in the blanks, and projects whomever and whatever is needed onto both the silence and the analyst. It's not a silence filled with the sexual attraction between us, not this time. It is a pure silence, wherein the energies present are obvious. There is some direct, wordless communication. If some words can be attached to it, they are probably: What I have done for you, you have done for me.

Eventually, without a word, we rise and hug, resting in the embrace for a moment. I walk out. My perception is bizarrely altered. Around the recessed halogen lighting in the hall, aureoles frisk and pulsate. The faraway objects grow in size as I move through the corridor, and change their aspect to meet me. The walls ripple with their inherent energy. I remember some effect like this on a university LSD trip, but this is more direct, gentler, and more matter-of-fact. This is what the wall and the furniture and the lights always are. Everything happens smoothly, without my interference, and seems to take both no time and forever.

In my car I lean my head on the steering wheel, feeling slightly unhinged. Absolutely anything might happen, without any control or safety. There is an underlying sense of risk.

Is this the way reality has always been? I suspect it is.

31. The Family

"When I arrived," Jason told Alexis, his wife, "I guess I was struck by the overall civilization of the airport. It was like any airport, with shops and cafés and everything, but more curry houses."

His family was strewn around his ample and comfortable living room, decorated over the years by pieces from their travels, and the best artwork given to him by his creative patients and that he could afford. A silver platter from Prague on the mantle, a wildly colorful Venetian lamp, its organic lines gracing the far corner of the room; a deeply polished mahogany coffee table from Germany. He had arrived home without a new piece this time, nor did he have one shipped. All he had was his story, and his nearly grown children and wife were gathered now to receive the offering.

"I think Pakistan is a deeply misunderstood country," said Alex, his eldest, prone to lecturing. He was reading history at St. Andrew's, in his third year, was home for the summer; he considered himself best placed for any informed political commentary. "The people of Pakistan in the vast majority practice a modern and inclusive kind of Islam. It embraces both the Shias and the Sunnis. But listen to the news, and you'd think they all were frothing-at-the-mouth fundamentalists, or else gun-crazy terror camp organizers." Alex leaned forward slightly from his sprawl on the over-stuffed armchair, ready for any riposte.

"Yes, I agree," said Jason, hoping to stop him before he really got going. It was his story, after all. "Everyone I encountered was just trying to get from A to B like any of us. Stacy is incredibly afraid of the Taliban, but a lot of people are more afraid of the warlords, so if the Taliban promise protection, they're all for the Taliban. And just about everyone is entirely cynical about the government. They have a lot of hope and optimism, it seems to me, for a people so patchily governed."

"How is Stacy?" asked Alexis, asking what she knew was the important question.

"My sister is hard to rattle," said Jason. "She seems very happy. She definitely *is* very happy with Hasid. She doesn't seem to mind any restrictions her life is under, but of course, she can work from home." Stacy wrote a column for The New Yorker magazine, *Inside the Hijab*, which the intelligentsia of North America ate up.

"I don't see how she does it," said Lydia, his youngest, still at secondary school, but heady with the new freedom of turning 18.

"She's absolutely fine," said Jason. "I don't think she had any illusions when she went out there. And quite frankly, she really likes playing housewife to Hasid and his family. She gets on with Hasid's mother better than she got on with our mother, which must help." He sighed, more worried about his calm and willful sister than he would ever admit. "Also, they're primed to leave at a moment's notice."

"I just wish they'd leave now," said Angela petulantly, his sweetest child, who was the artistic one, just switching from RADA to Brunel University, to his relief. "Misunderstood country or not. What a mess it all seems over there."

"Well," said Jason, itching to take the platform again, "you'll all be surprised to know that I was rescued by the

American Army at one point."

"But they're not even there!" retorted Alex.

"Indeed," agreed Jason.

Feeling like the Colonel, he regaled them with the story. The ledge, the void, the campfires dotting the valley; the hospitality, the crazy Colonel, the chase, the soldiers on borrowed leave, steeped in hilarity; his wonky turban, the better to hide his glorious crown of thick grey hair; his difficulties at the airport, his civilizing shower, and the patient, once delivered, now delivering. Dorothy menaced by the Wicked Witch of the West as she sought home, and Odysseus beset by many obstacles as he tried to return to Ithaca – neither of them a patch on *his* tale.

"Now I understand what Colonel Miller meant by 'a spot of bother,' said his wife, in her wound up tight voice, each syllable twang-twang-twanging, plucked on her last nerve by an unhinged harpist. "I was worried, but like always, your charm seems to have gotten you through." Alexis was pleased to be the ultimate possessor of a man so infamous for his charisma. She didn't have the usual problem with transferential patients, or the need to worm any unethical detail from him. Sometimes she wanted to know the rough percentage of patients who adored him, and if it was under 50%, she believed he was losing his touch. If she feared for him, she kept it to herself. Jason was fully human, yet fully invincible; her flawed champion, her antihero, Don Juan with a touch of Don Quixote.

"And what have you learned, Daddy?" asked Angela, teasing, parroting Jason's favorite parenting question.

"Ah! To conclude," he said in performance mode, "the whole adventure, and the exposure to a very different culture, didn't teach me a damned thing."

They laughed.

32. The Loss

The grief. I *am* the grief. There is no Lucy, there is everything; all of it colored with a knife-like sorrow. The thing that is missing is Jason, although the weekly visits carry on. No longer am I somehow inhibited by a sense that I must be well for him. The overwhelming realization, had frequently, is just how enormous, heavy and *total* the sadness is, and that I have never grieved before. I grieve my grandpa's death eleven years ago, I grieve the imminent loss of Jason, and I mourn my lost life; life wasted in active addiction, and some deeper loss of everything I'd ever thought important.

Alistair is patient again, takes me out to dinner, is attentive. If ever the small bundle of self needed validation, some proof of worth, I get it from him. After all the deception and neglect, he is with me, telling me over and over that I am valuable. Still, the grief is everything, and everywhere.

What is missing as well is some need to run away, have a drink, take some codeine, change the grief, stuff it away, get some relief. It is endurable. It is life on the front line.

Jason and I play together in a field, chasing each other, laughing. He moves well for a 50-something slightly overweight man who rarely exercises. He throws a clump of grass, hitting me squarely on the back of the head. We have always been playing, he hollers, and I make my way into an intriguing house on the edge of the meadow. Wandering from room to room, some under construction, one with a child peering at me from behind a heating vent, one flooded with sunlight, one dark and neo-Gothic, I finally find the bedroom of my childhood. A tin treasure box is on the dresser. "What you are looking for is what is looking" says the lid in raised letters.

I awaken in Jason's waiting area, thinking, there's no way I came up with that saying, it's too good. I must have read it somewhere. Jason appears, looking dapper and inviting as usual. He ushers me into his office.

"St. Francis," says the learned doctor when I ask him if he'd heard of it. "At least, I think that quote is usually attributed to St. Francis." He crosses his legs and smiles. The boundaries are depressing. There seems both no space between us and a universe, a huge distance that presence cannot conquer.

"Our penultimate session," I say, cutting to the chase. "Don't you *want* to see me anymore?" It is plaintive, just short of whiny, but not serious.

"I do," says Jason. "But you don't need me anymore. I have served my small purpose in the story of your life."

"I hate the idea of never seeing you again," I say.

"Lucy. Listen to me. I promise you, it will be all right. Just sit with that a moment," he continues, shrinkily. "It. Will. Be. All right."

"I believe you," I say.

We chew over Alistair's remarkable support, the resilience of the children, and the overwhelming nature of the grief. Jason agrees that I'm mourning my lost life. It peters out, and we wrap up and hug chastely.

"That hug sucked," I say, as we part, and he gives me the complex sideways amused-yet-serious look he always gives me after the hug. "We have one more session. By God, Jason, that last hug had better be good. A hug to carry me over a whole lifetime."

"No pressure then," he says, lightly. "I promise to do my very best," he adds quickly, suddenly meek as he sees the look I'm giving him.

33. The Disposal

There was calm. A sweet sense of peace pervaded the household. All the energy of all the thoughts generated by the household's denizens came together to form a warm ether, through which Alistair glided to the kitchen and grabbed a piece of cold pizza from the fridge. He ate it, man-style, still inspecting the contents of the fridge, door open, thoughtful, as he chewed and scanned for any tidbits he could scoff before they went off.

The fridge was, in fact, relatively empty. Jam, ham, leftover lamb, no more pizza – damn. His demographic precluded Spam. He grabbed the ham and closed the fridge, which had started its eco-beeping.

He sat at the kitchen table and noticed that *You Are All You See* was in a stack of cookbooks, left there from the morning planning session he'd had for tonight's supper, his weekly chance to shine in the kitchen. It was his (again stereotypically male) foray into cooking; ambitious, many courses, every pot used, every pan washed. He relished it. The newly enlightened Lucy still rolled her eyes and mopped up behind him, but was generous with her praise of the food he produced.

The book was still spookily following him.

He didn't really care anymore. He didn't understand it. He had come to realize that despite whatever the enlightenment freaks wrote about there being no right and wrong, they generally behaved fairly admirably, and that's what he cared about: behavior. He had realized somewhere along the way that he feared Lucy's behavior returning to what it was when she was using. He feared the financial instability, the deception, the neglect of the children. He knew all about addiction. He knew as long as she kept attending her meetings, it was likely that she would stay off the drugs and booze. And he knew that she was a good and sweet person, and that addiction made good and sweet people like Lucy do what appalled them. Then they became suicidal, and they asked their spouses for a divorce so they could go quietly away and murder their evil selves. He also realized that her therapy was instrumental in showing Lucy what a fantastic person she was, thus making the self-destruction less likely to return. He knew that Jason had accomplished this by loving Lucy, despite all the horrible details of her life that she confessed to him. He didn't care. At one point he felt insanely jealous, but now, he didn't mind at all.

The book, the awakening crap, he felt he didn't have to understand it. He knew he couldn't control anything more than he already was. He had covered all the bases as well as his ass, and his children's asses as well. Lucy was covering her own ass; nothing less than the Secret of Life was good enough for her, so determined was she to be well and whole and healed. And by God, he had to admire that.

My kids, he thought, are lucky. Not too many parents go to such lengths to ensure their fitness and worthiness as carers.

So, for old times' sake, he picked up the guru's tome and read:

'This is everything, this is wholeness, and there is nothing wrong. The mind's job is to rove and question and critique and

judge, conclude, and devise action. Yet whatever action is taken, whatever questions come up, whatever critiques and judgments are given, they are just what they are, not a solution to a non-existent problem. Yet even the perception of a problem is perfect. Every tool exists so that the somethingness from nothingness can be apprehended, and apparently negotiated. The notions that the appearance is flawed, and must be corrected, is part of the endless game; and although there is nothing wrong with wrong and nothing that needs changing, nor, indeed, anyone who can change the perfection of what is, it may be seen that this is paradise. It most assuredly, obviously is exactly what it is, and there is no way it could not be perfect, even in the questioning of its flawlessness. How beautifully it seems to appear, and it cannot be improved upon, even those confusing and ironic thoughts that long for improvement. This is what is longed for and searched for and killed for; this, this life, in this endless now, there is nothing to search for; this is it.'

Alistair walked to the pedal bin, opened it, and deposited the book within. The bin lid creaked back into place, sounding like hinges of a door in a haunted house.

Oh shit, he thought. I should have put it in with the recycling.

34. The Knife Revisited

It seems I can cook again.

"This is really good. Well done, darling," says Alistair, happy in his domestic bliss; the wife can clean *and* cook.

"Yes Mummy, it's delicious," says Max.

"Tasty, Mummy," says Florrie.

"No problem," say I, "and I'm sure you will all demonstrate your appreciation by doing the washing up."

"But we have homework," says Max.

"Lots of homework," Florrie chimes in supportively.

"What is that you were doing earlier then?" I ask.

"That was warm-up homework," Max replies, impressively deadpan.

They skulk off in a giggly fashion. Alistair and I exchange an age-old look: parental solidarity.

We clear the table in comfortable silence. As the last glass goes into the dishwasher, Alistair goes off to check on the kids' dedicated scholarship. I look at his familiar-yet-new face as he turns to go; I feel the lightness of great good fortune. My little family, yet not mine at all.

Why, I wonder, do they find the washing up so unpleasant? I don't really care if they help or not. I enjoy it, the whole process: the nice warm water, the bubbles; the smoothness of the plates; the satisfying grind of the garbage disposal, the sense of risk as it runs; the soft, absorbent tea towels polishing the glasses; the clink, as the glasses are set in the cupboard; the clank, as the plates are put on the shelf.

I fill the sink, move the tap left for some nice, hot water. Grab the washing-up bottle, nice big squirt, watch the bubbles rise. Lovely bubbles, each meniscus a convex rainbow prism. Lower the stack of plates. Gently secrete the cutlery into the water. Wash the knives first. The knife changes in my hands, and so does everything; although nothing really changes, and everything I ever thought important, everything I base my life on, everything I ever take seriously, melts away with the bubbles, cut by the knife.

35. The Last Session

Madness. I feel mad; the perception of no difference between myself and everything my senses sense; the feeling of being lived; the underlying riskiness of it all. Each bit of information has that unmistakable feeling of déjà vu: it has happened before; yet each moment is new, and each moment is indeterminate.

Jason and I sit as always in our last session. He is visually, energetically dynamic; he seems to dissolve into something like the snow on an old-fashioned television, and reappear, just the same, yet entirely unfamiliar. Some bit of my brain struggles to make sense of it, and keeps giving up. My body seems to have lost its edges. There is a settling; a little realization; this is how it has always been. Now, it is unfiltered.

"So, tell me," he says, and it is a bit like hearing an unfamiliar language, all cadence, rhythm and vowels. He said this at our first meeting.

"Something's happened, I think," I tell him, preparing myself to use wholly limiting words to describe the ineffable.

"They say, when it happens, you realize you've always been there," he says, seeming to know what I'm talking about. More déjà vu. Has he said this before, too?

"Or maybe it's always been there, and I've been in the way," I say.

"What's it like?" he asks, intrigued, slightly resistant.

"I can't describe it very well," I say, exasperated. "There's nothing different, not really. Everything I've been looking for is right in front of me, and always has been. But language is no use. It's not easy to even describe how an orange tastes, anyway," I say, falling back on Famous Quotations. "Coming here I felt like I was driving through myself... or something. Maybe it's like being lived." I sigh, flummoxed. "I have a huge urge to talk about it but I have no words. I was doing the washing up, and the knife I was holding seemed... just perfect. Exactly itself. I know that sounds daft. Then *everything* seemed just perfect. It still does. Oh, *I* don't know." I sit back, defeated by the task.

Jason leaned back in his chair as well. "We can stick to what we're doing here today," he says, letting me off the hook.

There was one of the pauses. He disappears, the room disappears. There was never anything there anyway. It seems exciting, but ordinary. The room thankfully stabilizes.

"Jason," I say.

"Yes, Lucy?" he answers.

"I want to thank you," I continue. "Forget about all this awakening crap for a minute. I was completely lost when we started. I had no idea what it was we were getting into. You've taken me from that, to having post-traumatic stress, to finally facing all the shit in my life and realizing it's all a gift." Huge waves of emotion roll by. "How can I thank you? There's nothing I can say or do. You've taught me how to live, how to have a relationship, through what we've done in here." I smile. "And what a relationship! Good, proper old-fashioned therapy, with extra added cuddles. Did we miss out any archetypes?

"Not too many," says Jason.

"Guru, lover, father, hero, rescuer, you've been them all."

"That's fine, if now you can see me for what I am," he cautions.

"You are Dr. Jameson, flawed person," I enthuse, "and you know, the therapy's always worked best when your humanity has come into it. If you hadn't loved me, I never would have believed I was worth anything."

"If you say so," he replies, circumspect.

"It's proper therapy, isn't it?" I say. "Just bog standard proper therapy, where you're everything to me. And it spreads. It's everything, that love. It's not just a feeling. I... hmmm." I shift in the chair, the pressure of it under my bum a little revelation unto itself. "There's no way to thank you for what you've done for me. My life is completely, utterly turned around. You've shown me how to trust, how to feel. I didn't feel anything before, I really didn't. Now I feel everything and I don't have to change it. Even if it sucks. I can live. Just live." We look at each other, and the therapy-wall collapses. "Thank you," I say, "thank you so much."

"You're welcome. You've helped me too, you know," he says.

"How?" I ask, insanely curious.

"Well, I can talk about any sexual feelings between me and patients more... unreservedly now," he says. "It's once again just a useful tool of therapy."

"I'll bet," I say, doubting there was ever a problem.

"And... broadly speaking," he continued, "the more I've helped you, in all the specific ways I've helped, the more you've helped me in the same ways."

That was it. That's all I was going to get out of him, but it's pretty fucking good.

"Do we finally get to have sex now?" he asks, deadpan.

"We're having sex like rabbits in some parallel universe," I say. "If we had sex in this universe, the fabric of reality would unravel."

"They say there are a lot of parallel universes," he says.

"The story can be as interesting as you like," say I.

"Well... perhaps it's time to end this particularly interesting story." He looks fleetingly sad, but I'm not sure. We rise.

"You're sure now," he says, "just once, right on the back of this chair?"

"We'll just have to make do with the hug," I say, overwhelmingly grateful for the joking, "but it'll have to be the best hug in the histories of all the universes."

The hug is awkward, slightly, and I come back for another, and fumble a bit gathering my belongings. Imperfect, and human; thus, perfect.

I drive home. Once there Florrie asks how my last session went; I've flagged it up for a couple of weeks.

"He said the story is now all about you guys," I tell her.

36. The Return

Here is Jason, or something very like him: the character Jason. And life flowed past him. He didn't change; his essence remained just the same, no matter what, and whatever that was, it was too simple to describe. It wasn't vision, or any of the senses; all the sensory information just rippled by. It wasn't even his thoughts or feelings; those, too, flowed past whatever it was, however intense or involving or important the thoughts and feelings were. Life appeared and reappeared in some endlessly fascinating form, and the character Jason seemed to make some use of it all, and interacted with it.

He wondered, briefly, if he was to be of any use to his patients. The next thought that came up was: does it matter?

His children were back at their various pursuits, 6th form, college, university; stuffing their heads full of what he and Alexis had conditioned them to believe was so terribly important. He felt the best father in the world. He knew they were just like him, life flowing by in its various guises, and they could come to him with the worst news of all – I've decided not to get my degree, Daddy. Daddy, I'm pregnant, and I'm marrying the father. Daddy, the drugs are too much, I've been expelled. He would love and accept, or maybe appear not to, and lessons would be learned or not, and he might refer one of them to a colleague for treatment; but he knew now that it was all the same thing.

He pulled into his space at the hospital and as he made his way to his office, made a call to a particularly troubled patient, who needed lots of support to get through a court case for cocaine. Jason reassured him, and the patient was grateful. Then he phoned his PA Rachel and told her the court date, to be sure his schedule allowed him to testify. Rachel met him in his office, and they continued the conversation smoothly in person, hanging up on each other as she opened the door.

Lisa, his wackiest client, was fragile and had been seen by his covering colleague six times in Jason's absence. Arnold, the chronic relapser, was back in hospital again. Jerry, mildly bipolar, had asked for an increase in his dosage of carbamazepine; and he had a new patient, Lucy Naughton, who had been admitted that morning. He hummed with pleasure at the opportunity to see Lu again; he remembered her from a few years ago, in rehab, a hotbed of potential stalled by addiction. He suspected that there were things she hadn't been ready to face then; such was often the case. And even though he knew she was perfect, complete and whole just as she was, as were all his patients, even the ones who suffered most – especially them – he found he was eager to help, or at least to try.

Nothing had changed.

37. The Conversation

Alistair and I, at great expense, go out. The babysitter alone is at least half the price of the meal. We are always a bit reluctant to splash out since the children's school fees take up what used to be expendable income. But I have to try and tell him what has happened, whatever the hell *that* is.

Midway through the main course I broach the subject. We are at a restaurant on the river. Cyclists and strollers pass by on the towpath; swans swim close with their teenage cygnets, almost as large as their parents but still grey and fluffy. Our fellow diners seem no different from ourselves, little lights at each table burning brightly, merging into the same light. I marvel at how I sit in a chair, amongst other small wonders. We eat, and I talk.

Trawling through the Internet, I tried to find some words to use earlier that afternoon. Advaita Vedanta, nonduality, consciousness, none of the websites seem to describe reality; I suspect words themselves are the difficulty. However, I am determined to try.

"I have to tell you something," I blurt.

"Great!" says Alistair, up for anything.

"I've had some kind of weird change of perception about reality," I continue, feeling like an idiot.

"You have?" he says; obviously, this isn't what he had expected.

"Well... I want to try and tell you about it," I say, fast losing courage.

"Please do." He leans forward. The pressure is immense.

"Hmmm. OK, well, you know, we're sitting here, on these chairs," I say, feeling more idiotic by the second.

"Yes." Patiently.

"Well, we're not really sitting on chairs. There's just sitting on chairs. No one's sitting. There is only sitting." It sounded just right when I read it on the website, but now I feel an absolute fool saying it.

"OK," he says, as someone to a lunatic who needs humoring. I plow ahead.

"This stuff we see... like the table, or you, or me... it's not here. It's like when you're dreaming, everything seems solid, but it's not. It's just the brain. It's just the mind, electrical impulses, synapses, all happening in the dark. It's like a hologram. It doesn't really exist."

Alistair gamely appears to think about it. "OK," he says finally, "I think I'm with you. It's science, really. The science of matter. Particle physics. The nature of matter itself, being energy, according to Einstein. Something like that."

"Something," I agree, pleased he is trying. Alistair, the businessman. "It's like, it doesn't matter. It's all just as it must be. Everything that seems to be around us, all the thoughts we have and the feelings, they're all just the same thing. All the things people hate, war, suffering; they're balanced by peace, and joy. Everything is perfect, it doesn't have to change, and actually it doesn't even exist. This idea that everyone has about making their lives work, it's just a story. The idea that we're alone, that we're separate from everybody else, is just not the case. Nobody has any free will, we're like... puppets. No matter how much free will we think we have, we don't. But knowing it's all a dream, an illusion or whatever, seems to take the burden out of it. Everything seems smoother, easier. But easier isn't the goal. There is no goal. Just existing is the goal." I take a deep breath. I've got the most radical stuff out. My story is all about not wanting Alistair to reject me. I await his response. There might be no time, and everything that happens just *seems* to in some everlasting moment, but there in the restaurant, time stands still.

Alistair goes through some extraordinary inner battle as he weighs up what I have said, and just how that might effect him, in his little world of working like a dog at a job he doesn't like for the betterment of his family. "What do you mean, nothing matters?" he asks, at last. "Nothing? Nothing *at all*? What, do you mean that now you might murder the children in their beds if I don't watch over you?" What an idiot, I think. Back to that nub of our conflict; back to he's the responsible one, I'm the raging addict loony; back to the worst case scenario, always at the fore of Alistair's thoughts, so that he may be better prepared to control any negative outcomes. Not, 'it doesn't matter as in the burden of life is lessened.' Not, 'whatever it is we have now, is whole and complete.' Not, 'any striving can be enjoyed for its own sake, not dependent on any certain outcome.' Not, 'oh my God, Lucy, what freedom you speak of!' Oh no, it's that I'm going to *murder the children in their beds.* What an idiot.

"Oh for Christ's sake, Alistair. Do you think I'm going to murder the kids? It's pretty unlikely, isn't it? I happen to love the little buggers." We've degenerated into a row, but it feels OK.

Alistair, a bit apoplectic, sputters on. "Do you mean that everything we've been working for together isn't important to you anymore? Why are we killing ourselves to get the kids through school? To live in a nice neighborhood? I can't keep it up all by myself," he says, and it is so plaintive, so informed by that underlying fear of the Void, of the possibility that all the hard work and effort are for nothing, that what felt like my heart melts, and I just want to reassure.

"Alistair, nothing's changed. Nothing's changed, except for the better. You see how I am now. I'm responsible, I'm able to just live, I don't have to run away from anything uncomfortable anymore. I'm here for you and the kids completely now. I'm so much more capable. Hell, I even may earn some money. Raising our kids as well as we can, that's the goal, never mind what I said. Nothing's different there."

It works. He seems reassured. We chat about the children, their traits, impending hormones and adolescence, and how proud we are of their achievements. And of ours. "You know," he says as we leave, stopping us as we enter the towpath; a cygnet gazes at us, unnoticed. "You're nuts, but I love you."

"I love you too, Alistair," I say. We hug.

I resolve to never try and speak to Alistair about enlightenment ever, ever, ever again.

38. The Patient

Jason sat at his desk after his PA left, readying himself to see a new patient, or at least fairly new; it had been three years since he'd last seen Lucy. He was remembering Lila, a patient he had a few years into practice. She was an inpatient at his hospital, admitted for a complete inability to cope with life, and yet there was nothing really wrong with her. She presented as a fantasist, infantile, unable to hold down a job or remember to turn off the iron; and yet she was embraced by, and embraced, the beauty and wonder of life. She saw angels, or some such creatures of light; she would stare transfixed at a flower for hours; she delighted in the presence of nearly everyone. There was nothing he could do for her that wouldn't destroy the wonder she was immersed in, and was a part of. There was no way he could activate her left brain without dulling the right brain's lack of organization and engagement with the moment. It was the saddest case of his career.

"Lila," he would tell her, "you are my sanest patient."

"You always say that," she would reply, with her little smile, the smile that hid the world's best secret. Lila kept the secret. He wasn't really able to help her.

But he loved her, in fact, she was his first foray into counter-transference. Onto her he projected all the children he had ever met, himself included; all the fools, all the archetypal nurturing women, all the gurus, his mother and sisters, all his lovers; and the desire to rescue her and look after her was intense. He, like all good therapists, did his best to use his potent humanity to show her the way; but Lila was never going to go forth in the world and negotiate reality successfully. She left the hospital eventually when her funds ran out. He wondered what had happened to her.

Every case, every single patient since Lila, was some attempt to make up for his failure with her. He was still in her thrall.

Another chance then, with Lucy.

His PA rang through with a phone call from Alexis; important, then, for she rarely if ever phoned him at work.

"Jason, darling," she said, sounding bereft. "Oh Jason. I'm so sorry, but I just got a call from your brother. Stacy, Hasid, the whole family, are missing. The neighbors say it doesn't look good, and part of the house has been burning. They just don't know what's happened." Tense, worried, she began to cry.

"Thanks Alexis," he said, "but I've got a patient waiting."

39. The Ultimate Twist

Surely there is some way to talk about this, to commu-
nicate the wonder of it without scaring or confusing
someone. I wasn't impressed with my attempts to tell Alistair
so, the veteran of 200,000 words of diary entries, I decide
to write it out. At least that way, in the story of my life that
seems to keep unfolding, there is some therapeutic value to
getting it out of my system. I scratch away, and read over my
first shot at it.

> *'Awakening is so simple. Enlightenment, or whatever you want
> to label it, realization as some call it, is simply what you are,
> right now. It's no different than what is happening – here,
> now. The thoughts that label whatever reality is for you, the
> thoughts that tell you that this isn't it, even they are it. The
> feelings that seem to be discontent or frustration, they are it too.
> Those thoughts that tell you that it couldn't be so simple... that
> it couldn't be any different than whatever it is you seem to have
> been experiencing all your life... they are what you are looking
> for. The thoughts that say "How could this possibly be it? This
> is boring!" Well, the boring-ness is it too, as are the thoughts
> that label it "boring". Those thoughts are just what's coming
> up in what you are. What you are is here and now. What you*

are is everything. What you are is not dependent on what your mind makes of it all. You will never be any closer to what you are than you already are. Those thoughts that it might be something different... those are it, too. Nothing is not it. Everything is what you are looking for. What looks is what you are looking for. Looking is what you are looking for. Here it is!'

My poor, overworked, beleaguered mind, with a snap-whirr-click, catches up with the everything-ness that I am trying to describe.

I have been doing it all along.

40. The Fire

Max was on the computer looking at nebulae. He had a school project on the Universe no less, and the size of it. Alistair looked over his shoulder as Max cut and pasted some gargantuan, unimaginable numbers that gave known reality's dimensions. He found a link to a YouTube video about the Hubble telescope, and a few pictures it had taken of some apparently dark, unremarkable corner of the sky; in it were thousands of discernible galaxies, millions of suns in each; in all likelihood, billions of planets. The narrator droned on about how small we were, and unimportant. Max, unawed, copied the link with satisfaction, his only goal a good piece of work that ticked all the boxes for his little class in his small school in his tiny town on puny Planet Earth, lost in the vastness of billions and trillions.

Alistair, similarly unmoved, had work to do. He got his phone from his pocket and settled down at the kitchen table to check his emails. One of his clients was being extremely unreasonable. The director of IT, who knew just what he wanted Alistair's software to do, refused to believe that not only would the software not do it, he also refused to believe that what he wanted was unnecessary. Alistair needed to call a meeting with the head of purchasing, who was much more realistic; the techies, who could explain why it wouldn't do what the IT director wanted it to do; and the COE, who would explain why it wasn't necessary for it to do that. Alistair was a good director, coordinating the deal-making players until everyone was absolutely gagging to buy his company's software. He enjoyed it; he wasn't like Lucy, who had almost perished with the need for life to be much more than it already was. Alistair enjoyed his lot, the challenging job, the demanding kids, the difficult wife.

His eye fell on the counter near the table, below the glass-fronted cupboards where the glassware was kept. Under a bowl of fruit, like some boomeranging specter of doom, was the nonduality book. Undoubtedly Lucy had rescued it from the rubbish for some wry and wifely reasons. Zombie-like, he reached for it, opened it, and read:

'Such a lot of complicated mess everywhere. Such a lot of bother and to-do in order to get anything done. There's nothing wrong with that, but there it is. The mind boggles at the simplicity of this message. It just doesn't seem right, that there is nothing to be done, no one doing it, nowhere to go. The mind will string along the apparent happenings into a story, and doesn't like the idea of not being in charge. According to the mind, it all will happen later. Subtle procrastination born of a feeling of un-worthiness causes untold wretchedness. Perhaps this is "good" news then – there is no real procrastination. The goal is met, even in the midst of that uncomfortable feeling of mixed regret and hopelessness, that mix of the perfectionism that quells the birth of endeavor and the fear that it won't be worth the effort. Maybe if this is seen, then life seems lighter, and though this is likely, there are no guarantees. Perhaps if there is nowhere to go and no one to get there, every obstacle dissolves. Goals seem to arise and the apparent actions that ensue can be loved for their intrinsic value, not their magical curative properties, the malaise being the sense of pointlessness and meaninglessness. The mind won't see it, but this is enough. Simply what is, is

enough. More than enough, more than the mind can fathom. Beingness loves being, and that is enough, for it is everything.'

Alistair picked the book up with his index finger and thumb by a corner of the front cover. Keeping it at arm's length, he took it to the living room, where he released it onto the floor. Although it was mid-spring, he built a fire in the art-deco fireplace, using a whole box of extra-long matches as overly-effective kindling. There was no wood or coal, so he raided the toy cupboard and used a Jenga set and some old, long unused wooden train tracks to build up the fire; as he recalled, he had hit the ceiling when Lu had told him how much the train set cost, but now he didn't care. When the fire was going steadily he placed the book on top and watched it, rarely blinking, until it was reliably a pile of ash.

NON-DUALITY PRESS

If you enjoyed this book, you might be interested in these
related titles published by Non-Duality Press:

The Light That I Am, J.C. Amberchele
Awake in the Heartland, Joan Tollifson
Painting the Sidewalk with Water, Joan Tollifson
Only That, Kalyani Lawry
The Wonder of Being, Jeff Foster
An Extraordinary Absence, Jeff Foster
Awakening to the Dream, Leo Hartong
Dismantling the Fantasy, Darryl Bailey
Standing as Awareness, Greg Goode
The Transparency of Things, Rupert Spira
Ordinary Freedom, Jon Bernie
I Hope You Die Soon, Richard Sylvester
The Book of No One, Richard Sylvester
Be Who You Are, Jean Klein
Who Am I?, Jean Klein
I Am, Jean Klein
The Book of Listening, Jean Klein
Spiritual Discourses of Shri Atmananda (3 vols.)
Nobody Home, Jan Kersschot
This is Always Enough, John Astin
Oneness, John Greven
What's Wrong with Right Now?, Sailor Bob Adamson
Presence-Awareness, Sailor Bob Adamson
You Are No Thing, Randall Friend
Already Awake, Nathan Gill
Being: The Bottom Line, Nathan Gill

For a complete list of books, CDs and DVDs, please visit:
www.non-dualitypress.com

Forthcoming books from NON-DUALITY PRESS
2011

THE ALMIGHTY MACKEREL AND HIS HOLY BOOTSTRAPS
by J.C.Amberchele
The headless perspective

THE TELLING STONES by Riktam Barry
Enlightenment, the spirit of the '60's and modern times

GONER by Louis Brawley
The last five years with UG Krishnamurti

ESSENCE REVISITED by Darryl Bailey
Slipping past the shadows of illusion

THE LOVING AWARENESS IN WHICH ALL ARISES
by Rick Linchitz
Dialogues on awakening

BLESSED DISILLUSIONMENT by Morgan Caraway
Seeing Through Ideas of Self

THE LAST HUSTLE by Kenny Johnson
Finding true happiness and freedom in prison

THE PLEASANTRIES OF KRISHNAMURPHY
by Gabriel Rosenstock
Revelations from an Irish ashram

DRINK TEA, EAT CAKE by Richard Sylvester
Dialogues and observations of a tour in Germany

CONSCIOUS.TV

CONSCIOUS.TV is a TV channel which broadcasts on the Internet at www.conscious.tv. It also has programmes shown on several satellite and cable channels. The channel aims to stimulate debate, question, enquire, inform, enlighten, encourage and inspire people in the areas of Consciousness, Healing, Non-Duality and Psychology.

There are over 200 interviews to watch including several with communicators on Non-Duality including Jeff Foster, Steve Ford, Suzanne Foxton, Gangaji, Greg Goode, Scott Kiloby, Richard Lang, Francis Lucille, Roger Linden, Wayne Liquorman, Jac O'Keefe, Mooji, Catherine Noyce, Tony Parsons, Halina Pytlasinska, Genpo Roshi, Satyananda, Richard Sylvester, Rupert Spira, Florian Schlosser, Mandi Solk, James Swartz, and Pamela Wilson. Some of these interviewees also have books available from Non-Duality Press.

Do check out the channel as we are interested in your feedback and any ideas you may have for future programmes. Email us at info@conscious.tv with your ideas or if you would like to be on our email newsletter list.

WWW.CONSCIOUS.TV

CONSCIOUS.TV and *NON-DUALITY PRESS*
present two unique DVD releases

CONVERSATIONS ON NON-DUALITY – VOLUME 1

Tony Parsons – *The Open Secret* • Rupert Spira –
The Transparency of Things – Parts 1 & 2 • Richard Lang –
Seeing Who You Really Are

CONVERSATIONS ON NON-DUALITY – VOLUME 2

Jeff Foster – *Life Without a Centre* • Richard Sylvester –
I Hope You Die Soon • Roger Linden – *The Elusive Obvious*

Available to order from: www.non-dualitypress.com